Following Our Celtic Call

A Pilgrimage in the West of Ireland & Newgrange
with Paintings and Poems

Celtic Blessings and Energy to you!
Patty Smitherman

May your Blessings Abound!
Kathleen Michaud

Patty Wheeler Smitherman   **Kathleen Dyer Michaud**

Copyright © 2019 Patty Smitherman & Kathleen Michaud
All rights reserved

ISBN-13: 978-1-7329964-0-3

Dedication and a Blessing

We dedicate this book to Seekers everywhere:

You who have a hunger for Meaning;

You who long for Truth;

You who can laugh with Delight.

Dear Reader,

As You absorb this book,

May the words inspire you to sit in Nature,

>feel the warmth of her soul and drink in her spirit.

May the images cause your heart to open,

>to look for beauty

>and to be a pilgrim

>on the way to deeper understanding.

May it carry you to others who are rich in Celtic soul.

May you find what you need for inspiration

>to clothe and support you

>on your soul's pilgrimage.

Acknowledgments

We are grateful to the many people who helped us bring this book to life.

We thank our husbands, Fran Michaud and Marshall Smitherman, who have advised and encouraged us. Humble thanks especially to Fran Michaud who did yeoman work shepherding us through the formatting jungle.

We are so grateful to Dr James Flannery for his time, Celtic wisdom, and unwavering support.

Thank you, Josh Langston: you edited cleverly and with good humor.

To our Wisdom Seekers Book Group and Mary and Martha's Place friends: we are so grateful for those thoughtful conversations, for opportunities to present workshops, and for your insightful feedback.

Kathy: I have benefited from wonderful watercolor teachers, Karen Bradshaw and Tom Lynch, and a soul friend Spiritual Director, Stephanie Visokay.

Patty: Many thanks to Melissa Helton for your poetic insights and constructive criticism.

“Celtic Spirituality is above all a spirituality of place….”
Esther De Waal

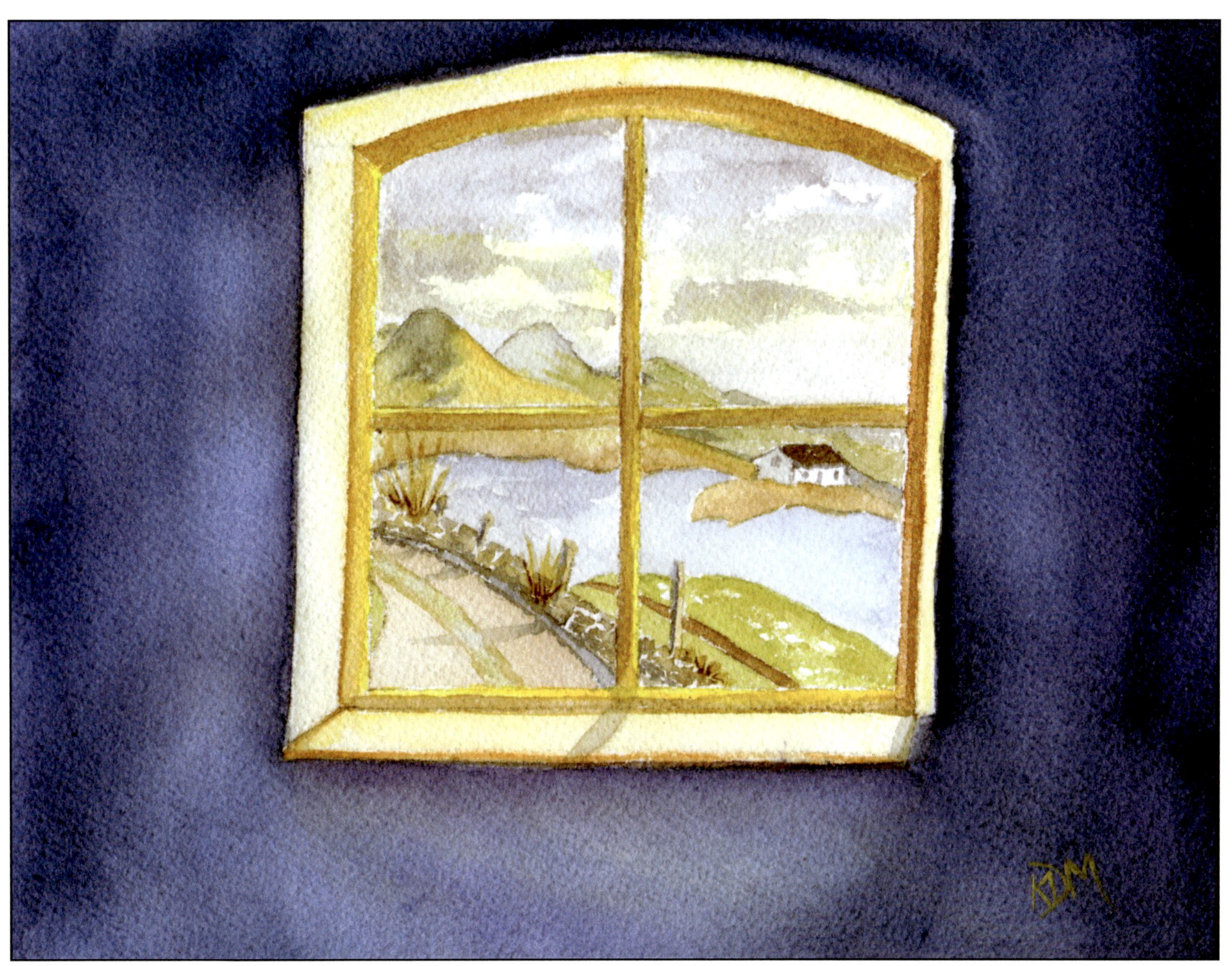

Table of Contents

Introduction

This is a book about adventure. The adventure includes learning, loving and taking risks. It's about living life in a more robust way.

We hope to introduce you to a deep, transformative, personal experience using our responses to the land where Celtic Christian Spirituality blossomed during the fifth through seventh centuries CE.

Although the term Celtic Spirituality means many things to many people, it was not an organized religion per se (Woods, *Celtic Spirituality*, disc 1). Ireland, the most remote edge of the known western world, was never conquered by Rome, and is no stranger to beauty or hardship. While sharing a common Christianity with continental Europe, Irish practices and sensibilities differed. Pre-Christian influence by the Druids, clan rivalries, the rise of monasticism, Vikings appearing on the horizon to pillage, wild wind and weather all contributed to the religious sensibilities that grew in Ireland and later Scotland and Wales. Ireland is also the land of stories, songs, generous hospitality and a daily lived devotion to the spiritual. A culture developed here where men and women were often equals, and every action had its accompanying blessing.

Late in the 19th century, Alexander Carmichael collected the Gaelic oral traditional prayers and blessings of the rural Scottish farmers and fishermen. The voluminous *Carmina Gadelica* was published in 1900, thus saving these prayers from extinction. John Philip Newell points out that these prayers were used locally by both Protestants and Catholics over the generations (Newell, J.P. *Celtic Prayers from Iona*, p.5-6). By the 1990s, several lyrical and knowledgeable authors were publishing on this topic. The doors of possibility had swung open for us. Possibility led to dreaming. Dreaming led to conversations. Change was in the wind. For over twenty years we had been absorbing these "new" ideas and engaging in the spiritual practices of thoughtfully walking the land, meditating daily, pursuing creative projects in writing and painting, and seeking out meaningful conversations. And, so, the dance continues.

 In this book, we will explore three themes: (1) the Celtic love of the natural world and her cycles, an Incarnational Spirituality, (2) weaving old and new ideas into dedicated lives lived with love of beauty and learning; aware that the Divine is always near, (3) the Celtic ability to be at ease holding and "fusing diverse elements" (Duncan, A. *Celtic Mysticism*, p.7). For example, there is the tension of light and darkness or action and waiting which necessarily include the liminal spaces of thresholds.

Going Deeper with This Book

When was the last time an image captured your imagination?

When was the last time you exclaimed "wonderful"?

When was the last time something opened up deep inside you?

Here is our invitation to you: Expect to be surprised with what arises in reading our book.

To Begin:

Set a time and place where you are comfortable. You may want to light a candle. Have your journal available. Breathe three deep cleansing breaths. Center. Follow these suggestions for reading a poem or studying a painting.

Tips for reading a poem:

Read the poem aloud. Listen for a word or phrase that "pops" for you.

Sit quietly, holding the word or phrase in your heart.

Listen for what shows up. Write the word or phrase in your journal and then your own thoughts about it.

Inviting the painting to speak:

Close your eyes. Then gently open them, keeping them unfocused. Don't think too much.

Focus on an image or color in the painting. Which one speaks to you or chooses you?

Hold that color or image in silence. Write a brief description of your experience in 2-3 sentences.

Our experience in the West of Ireland was deeper and more meaningful than we anticipated. As we went about absorbing the spirit of the place, we slipped deeper into an ancient world. May you too experience the deep beauty that resides in you!

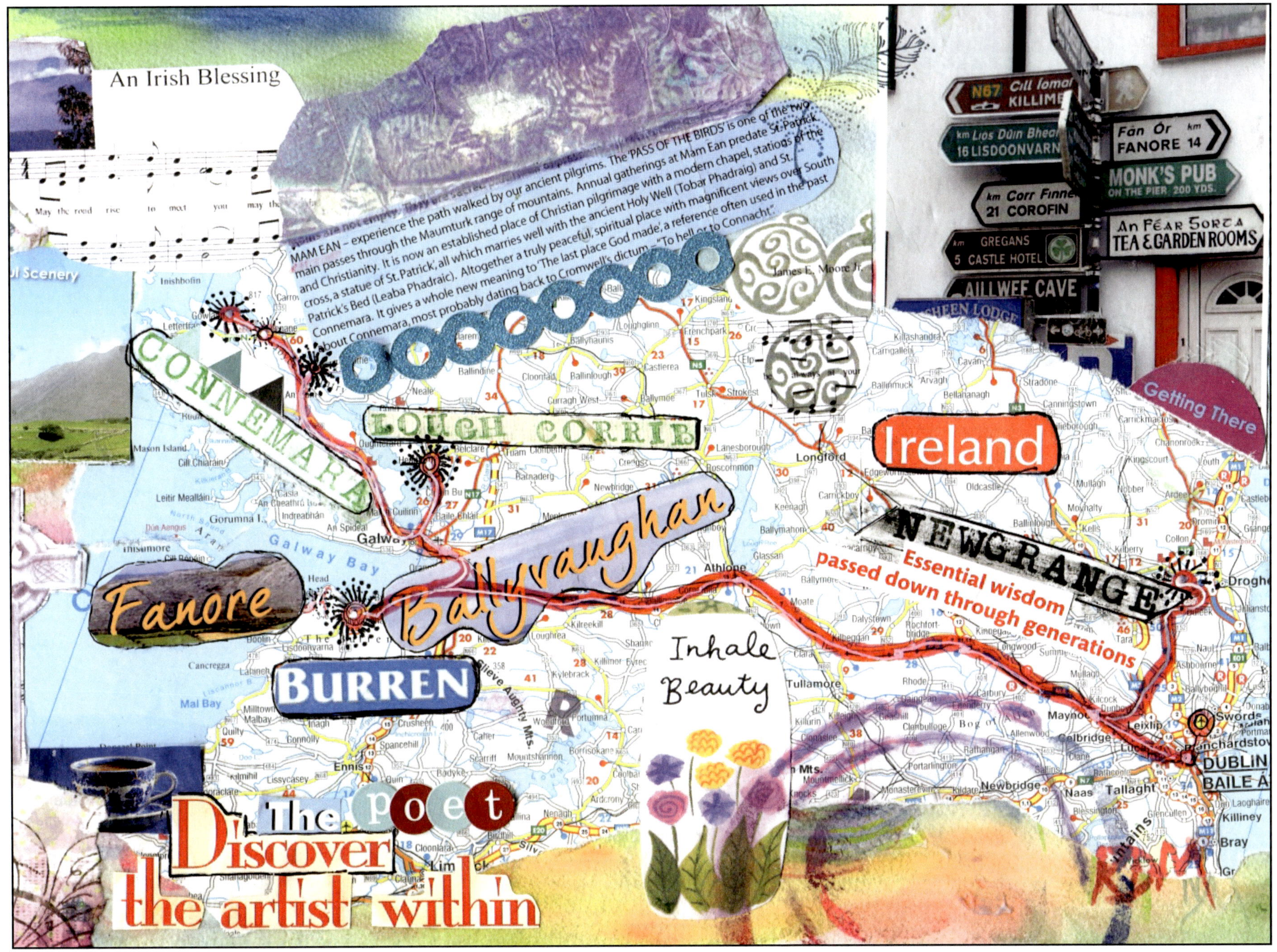

An Irish Blessing
May the road rise to meet you may the
MAM EAN – experience the path walked by our ancient pilgrims. The 'PASS OF THE BIRDS' is one of the two main passes through the Maumturk range of mountains. Annual gatherings at Mam Ean predate St. Patrick and Christianity. It is now an established place of Christian pilgrimage with a modern chapel, stations of the cross, a statue of St. Patrick', all which marries well with the ancient Holy Well (Tobar Phadraig) and St. Patrick's Bed (Leaba Phadraic). Altogether a truly peaceful, spiritual place with magnificent views over South Connemara. It gives a whole new meaning to 'The last place God made', a reference often used in the past about Connemara, most probably dating back to Cromwell's dictum - "To hell or to Connacht".
James E. Moore Jr.
CONNEMARA
LOUGH CORRIB
Ireland
Fanore
Ballyvaughan
NEWGRANGE
Essential wisdom passed down through generations
BURREN
Inhale Beauty
The Poet
Discover
the artist within
N67 Cill Iomai KILLIMER
km Lios Dúin Bhean 16 LISDOONVARN
km Corr Finne 21 COROFIN
km GREGANS 5 CASTLE HOTEL
AILLWEE CAVE
Fán Ór km FANORE 14
MONK'S PUB ON THE PIER 200 YDS.
An Féar Gorta TEA & GARDEN ROOMS
Getting There

The Pilgrimage Begins

In late October 2016, after renting a car in Dublin, we two set out, going west toward Galway, holding our breath as Kathy relearns driving on the left side of the road. Of course, we get lost right away. That is when we realize we really are on a pilgrimage, not a trip.

We are friends of different religious traditions who have never traveled together. Kathy is of Irish Catholic descent and feels a deep connection to this land. These watercolor paintings (and now writings) come out of a love of the land of her heritage, Ireland. Patty is from Scots-Irish stock with farming and music flowing in her veins. The thrill and challenge of putting words to deeply felt experiences will be her companions during this pilgrimage.

We have prayed about this trip, hoping to have some transformative personal experiences that we can share through paintings and poems. We trust that we will be responsive to the Spirit; that we will meet who we ought to meet; that we will see what we ought to see. As we set out, this pilgrimage is all about being open and trusting. To that end, we only make B&B reservations in four places.

Here, in Dublin's outskirts, is our first challenge. Going in circles in the warehouse section of Dublin, certainly not a beautiful location, we summon up our collective creativity and sense of humor. It is true that a pilgrimage includes a series of challenges or tests. Also, a pilgrimage has an intention. Finally, a pilgrimage may look linear on the map, but is more often circular in experience. Where do you turn when lost and facing an oncoming ten-wheel truck on a narrow street with a parked car beside you? Where do you turn when all the while the highway is in view, but inaccessible?

Courage, which comes from the French for "heart," is required when following the sometimes paradoxical prompts of spirit. Different varieties of courage are called out in different situations. Some courage is outright bravery. Some courage is clever. Some courage is just showing up. We show up! The good news is that we don't die crashing into the truck. Our rental car still has both mirrors. Mysteriously, a sign for the highway appears at a moment when we can turn as it directs. We finally find our way to the M6 West, both humbled and elated to be on the road to the beauty of the Burren. We two pilgrims are ever so grateful and humble with all our senses alert.

The Burren
Land of Stark Contrasts

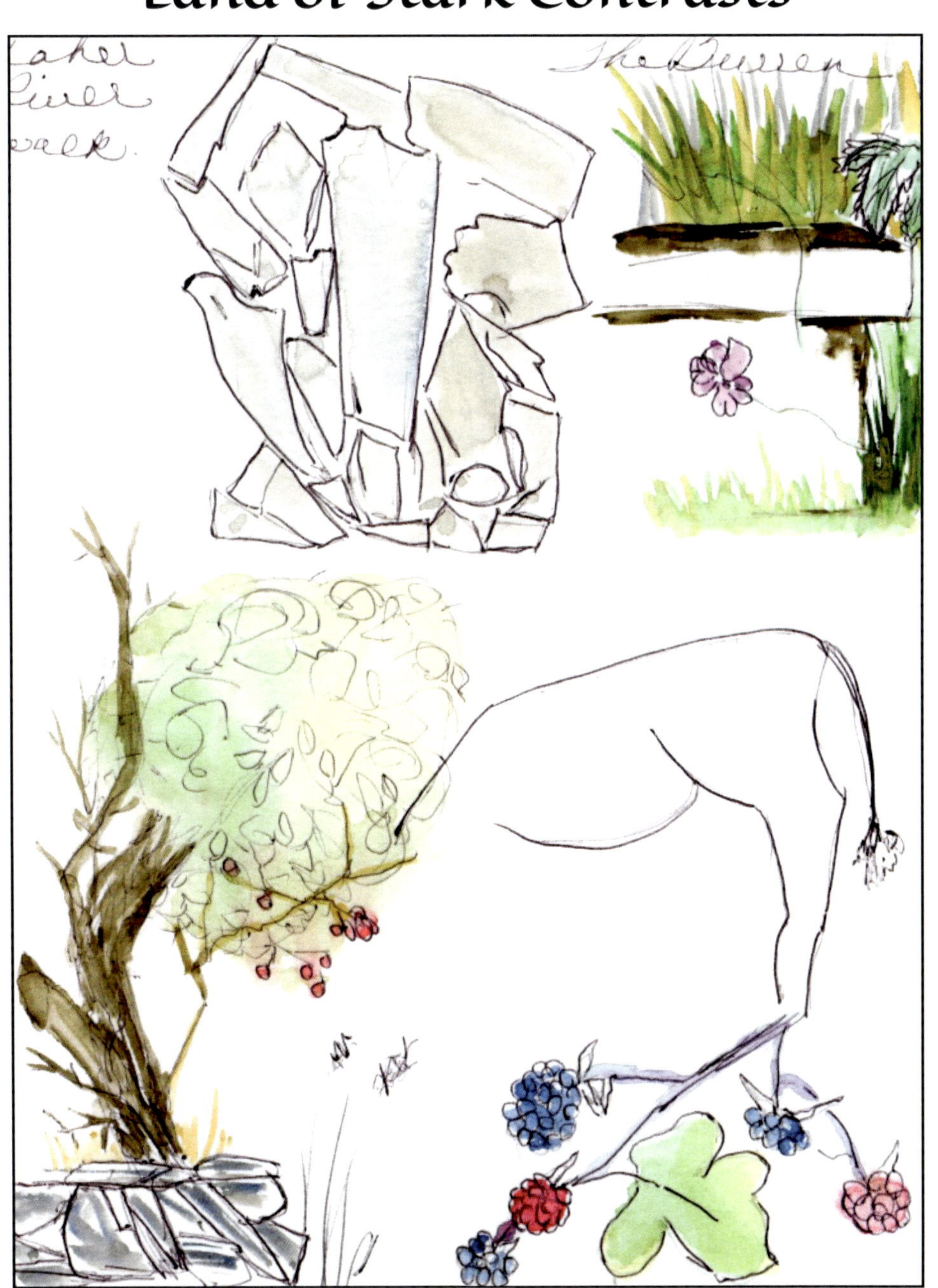

In this limestone land of rock upon rock, how can you survive if you don't share?

The genius of the Irish is that, with rugged scarcity all around, they excel in hospitality, sharing and song.

The Burren is surprising. Not many earthly places have layers of blue black rock that go on for miles. Not many places have "glacial erratics" either. At first view, the severe Burren takes our breath away, literally.

The many miles of stone walls that crisscross the Burren give us pause. They are reassuring in a way. How many lives of labor do they represent? How many centuries? No fertile fields are visible, only rocks, rocks, rocks.

Kathy's forefather, Stephen Connolly, immigrated to the United States during the Potato Famine. He was a gardener on a Boston estate, also working with stones in the rocky Massachusetts soil. Later, his sons and grandsons became stoneworkers, building roads and foundations for the wealthy. The construction company they founded is still run successfully by her cousins today. Body cells have memory. Maybe that is why this land and these rocks are affecting her so deeply. We remember the call of home, both ethnically and spiritually.

Later, by surprise, while we walk along the little Caher River road, we spy grasses, daisies, ivy, and brambles. We hike. Back into the Burren we go, and there are the fields and pastures of green, all sorts of greens. Patty keeps exclaiming, "How fertile this soil is here!" Her roots in Alabama's farmland recognize the good rich farmland here. There are what look like very happy cows. What a feast for the eye and heart! What a study in contrast!

Intense Thresholds

Look at the water

creating a threshold divide

from beach to mainland,

from wild boisterous Atlantic

of high waves, stormy torments

to solid implacable Burren,

the limestone kingdom.

Nestled near this transitional line

the St. Patrick church endures,

- solid, unadorned, unprotected -

a second liminal space where the Transcendent Mystery

rests our weariness, "waits to bless and heal us"

sings us into joy,

the joy of rocks, sand, water, green pastures,

Atlantic, Burren beauty.

Poet's Notes: *After our first wander in the Caher Valley, we went down to Fanore Beach near the end of the Caher River. Somehow it was not appealing to me. I thought the beach bland-colored but Kathy saw more. And, she brought about the encounter there with Aisling, a River Dancer and London artist, by asking about and admiring Aisling's little dog. Somehow I was locked up inside and wonder now why. Aisling broke the lock with her Celtic spirit and the invitation to visit her mother's art gallery further south on the Wild Atlantic Way. The painting of St. Patrick's church shows my favorite perspective – looking back into that fascinating valley and then pondering thresholds, so important in Celtic spirituality.*

Intense Thresholds

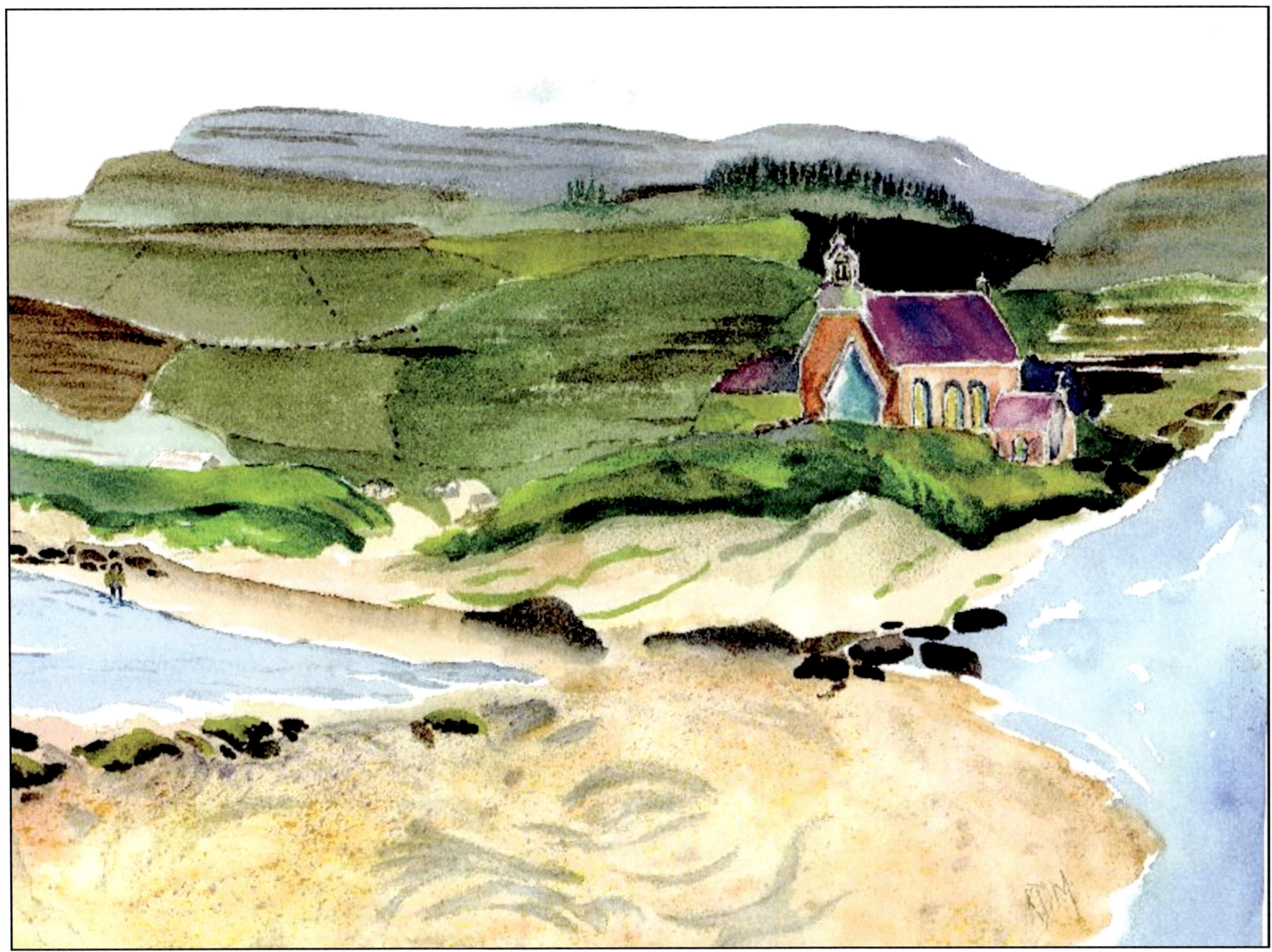

Artist's Reflection: *Walking down the steep path to Fanore Beach, a friendly little dog guides us. Curving, rocky, sandy; it feels like a passage. Will we need boots? There are feather patterns of black sand here- surprise. Curling moss swirls from the ever present, rolling ocean. And this is where we meet Aisling (a dream or vision), a River Dancer.*

St. Kevin and the Blocked Gate

For Dr. James Flannery

I hold something precious.

    like a St. Kevin, I stand with arms outstretched

    at the threshold of two opposites.

This, the farm track down a Burren mountain,

    muck, dead leaves, bare ground

There, the lush pasture within stone walls.

At a blocked gate between both domains,

I stand quite still, hoping for,

even willing, that this imaginary blackbird's egg I hold

will, like a necessary third force,

be a catalyst at this threshold of imagination

    between decay

    and promise

creating a fourth, a winged arising,

a healing, a new beauty.

Poet's notes: *We had parked the car on the Caher Loop Trail, just off the Caher Valley dirt road. Kathy set-up to paint near this gate. There was something about the gate that was sad. An opening, a possibility closed? I was intrigued with Seamus Heaney's poem, "St. Kevin and the Blackbird" which I heard Dr. James Flannery read beautifully. I began to imagine St. Kevin healing the blockage of this wounded gate and Teilhardian evolution of something beautiful.*

Blocked Thresholds

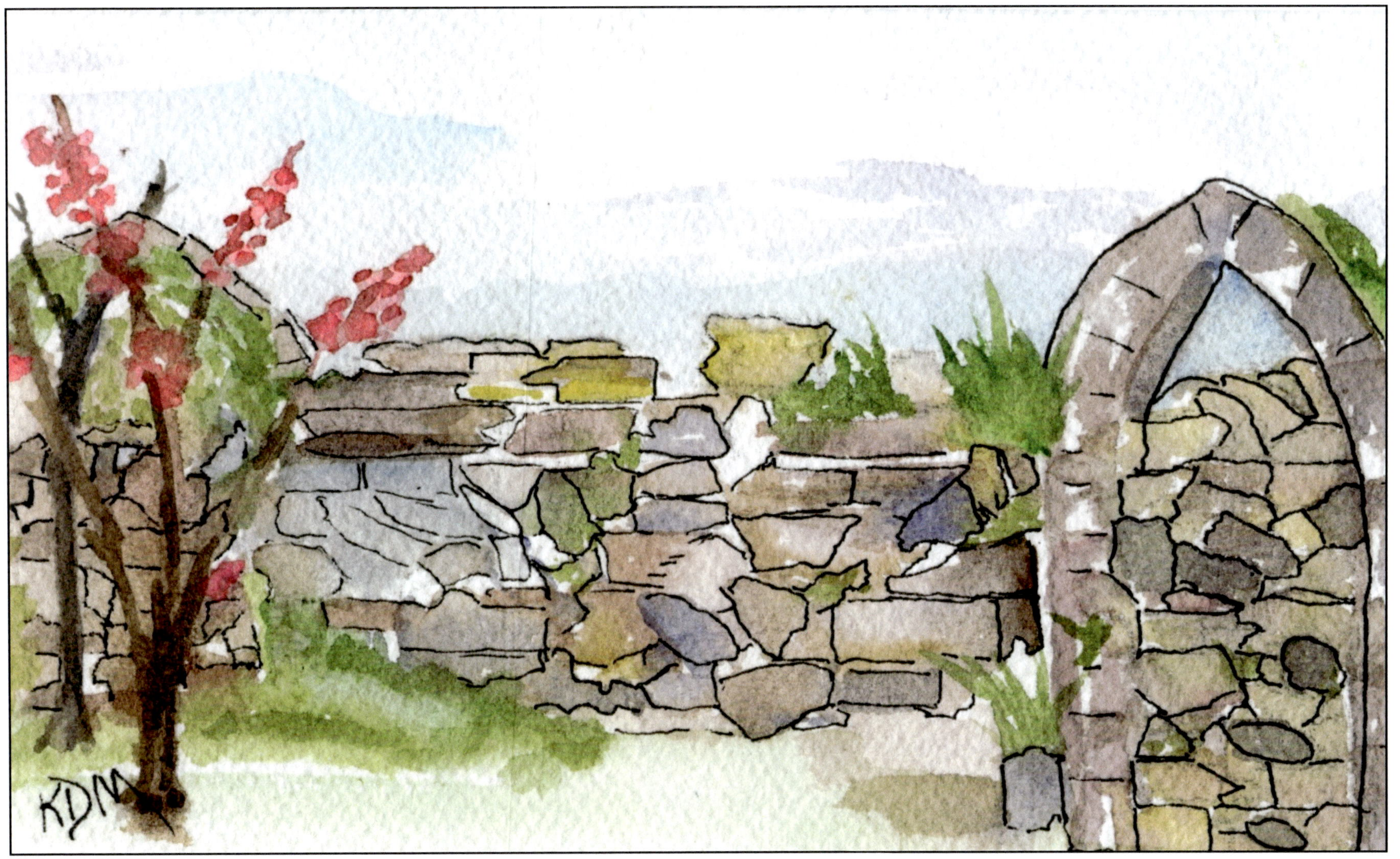

Artist's Reflection: *It caught my eye immediately. A blocked threshold built into a rock wall. What happened here? Why block off these arched entries? When the way is blocked, what happens to a person? Yes, there is grief and anger. There also can be an invitation to fly higher, or think differently. I imagine resilience appearing as a guardian angel of possibilities. I notice the clear space at the top…hope.*

Attention

Nestled in wet grasses
    clinging to a single stalk,
    dry among such viriditas,
A tiny snail, white with purple spiral,
    watched over by wild daisies.

Easily missed in this lavish landscape
    but once seen, snails multiply.
They are everywhere,
    little spiral jewels that proclaim
    this river valley full of riches,
    treasures everywhere,
    thin purple spirals that call us to pause,
    put on our awareness vision,
    look slowly and calmly for
    spiral snails, lichen mandalas, heart-shaped rocks.

We open our eyes to wonder
    at the natural arising of the spiral,
    Celtic symbol of sun energy,
    whirling, driving cosmic force.
    And there is the little snail holding all this meaning
    for artists and mystics
    who find treasure in the harshly beautiful Burren.

Poet's Notes: *While Kathy painted on the Caher Loop trail, I just wandered off, telling her I'd be somewhere back down the valley road. I was feasting visually as I slowly sauntered, not wearing my glasses. I saw a little white circle on a stalk in the grasses on the side of the road. Putting my glasses on, I discovered it was a little snail with a purple spiral. Then I began to discover them everywhere – by paying attention! I was astonished and wrote the poem following Mary Oliver's sage advice.*

Daisies and Snail

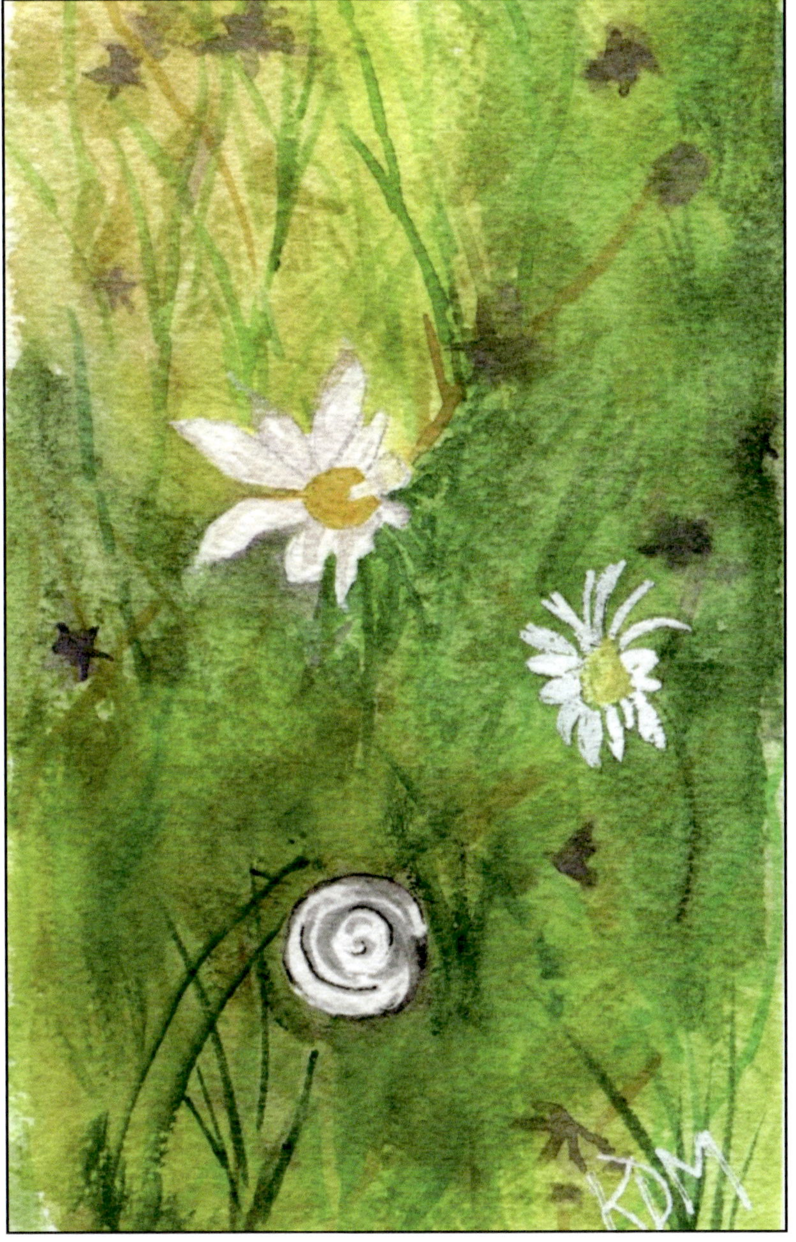

Artist's Reflection: *Nodding and bobbing on the slender grass, the perfect snail goes about its business witnessed by the friendly daisies. There's a little community here under the Burren brambles. Walking has allowed us to notice and celebrate. I think of the play on words between "soul" and "sole."*

Ochre Surprise in the Burren

Red fall berries have an energy frequency
  that fillets out red and
  bounces it back to the eye.

In the Burren in the fall
  green light fills the eye,
  green bouncing back from rock crevices
  where mosses and grasses valiantly grow,
  then the wonder of hidden pastures,
  shining thick, green, damp and wondrously lush
  all from Ireland's sun, rain and constant moisture.

The limestone rock beams gentle gray and white,
  red, dark red comes from berries
  then blackberry black shining and offering
  sweetness from brambles.
The water of the Caher shimmers green and bright
  and cascades white.

And on nearby rocks, a surprise,
  circular lichen,
  orange and ochre,
  mandalas of unlikely color in this
  beloved valley of green, green, green, gray-white,
  occasional red-berry punctuation and these,
  orange and ochre suggestions of rose windows,
  Celtic Crosses, here on stones, near the Caher.

Poet's Notes: *This color was a surprise, a color that wasn't common in the Burren. It was almost hidden among the rich greens of grasses and brown-grays of rocks. The lichen were small but the shape– something spiritual, a mandala of sorts. I wonder if I would have seen it if I hadn't taken a wander with no objective in mind other than being awake to the world around me.*

Primal Fungi

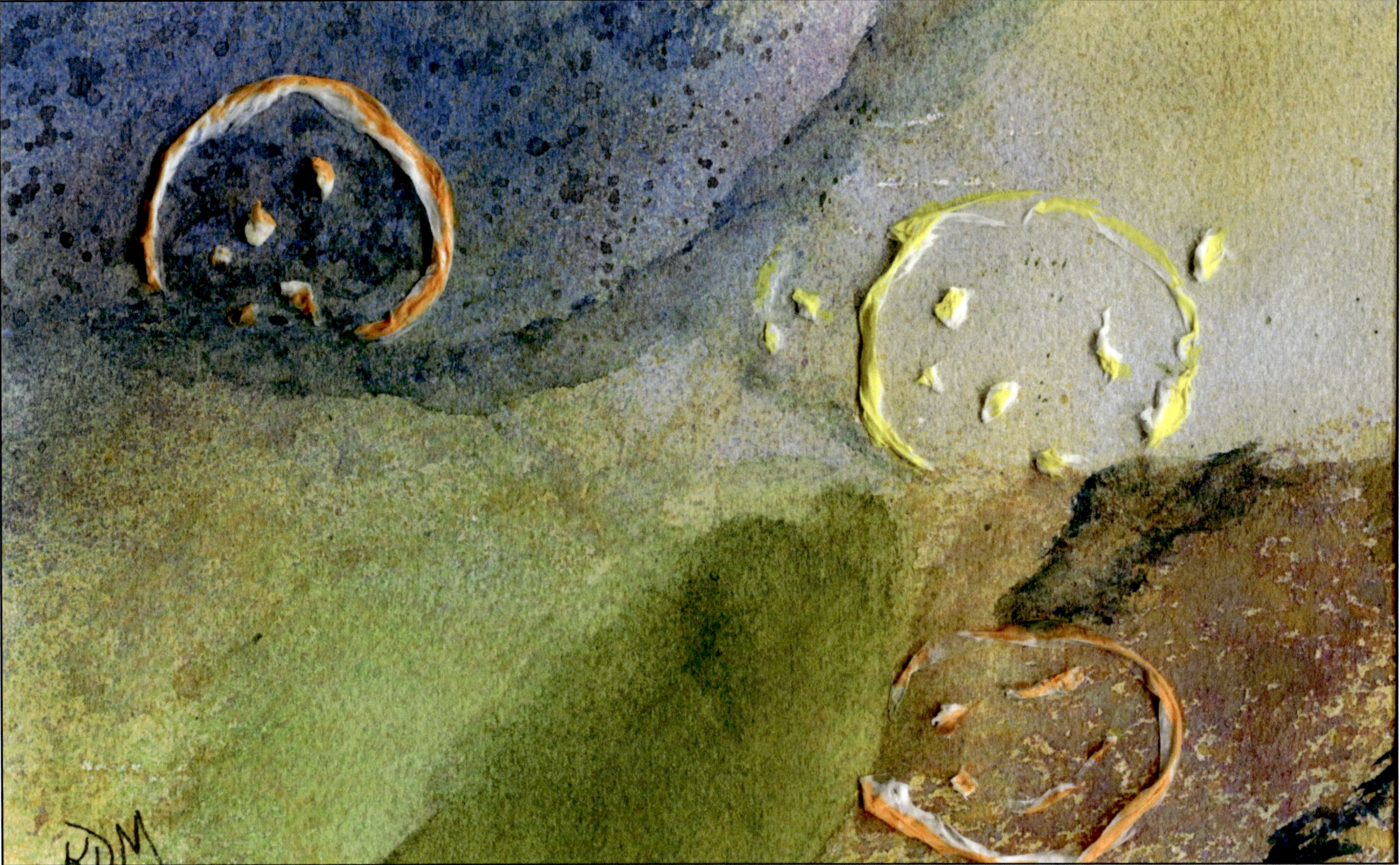

Artist's Reflection: *What in the world? Is there no end to the surprises in this riverscape? Ancient peoples put their trust in nature's observed patterns. And here on these rocks are the circles-spirals. Bright orange and lemon-yellow circles of fungi are a primal motif saying, "Notice! Pause, there's something important for you to understand about the big cycles of life on this planet." As dependable as solid rock, these fungi have more to say about a way of life. There are energies. Orange is for sexuality, joy, even compassion. Yellow is for energy, fire. Some invisible power is at work in this world. Some graces lifted the veil and people began to see…and then told us what they saw in words and art.*

Wild Callings

The calls come in thunderous pounding
   grabbing the shore and then retreating
   pulling back to the sea to prepare
   for another booming groom's entreaty,
   Come, Beloved! Come!

The powerful roar calls the little Caher
   to race - trickling, swirling, singing its bride song,
   crashing over rocks with lacy veil of spray
   rushing forward, downward
   through the Burren's beautiful Caher Valley
   protected by green pastures of wonder,
   watched over by attendants -
   white horses on the ridgetop.

The Caher River rushes on, in response
   to insistent ocean callings,
   to union with the Wild Atlantic.

Poet's Notes: *The Atlantic is a powerful force in Western Ireland and a resource. Its waves pound the cliffs and shores and its storms can be fierce. Then there is the little Caher River joyfully running down from the upper Burren to join the sea, thus the idea of union.*

Caher River

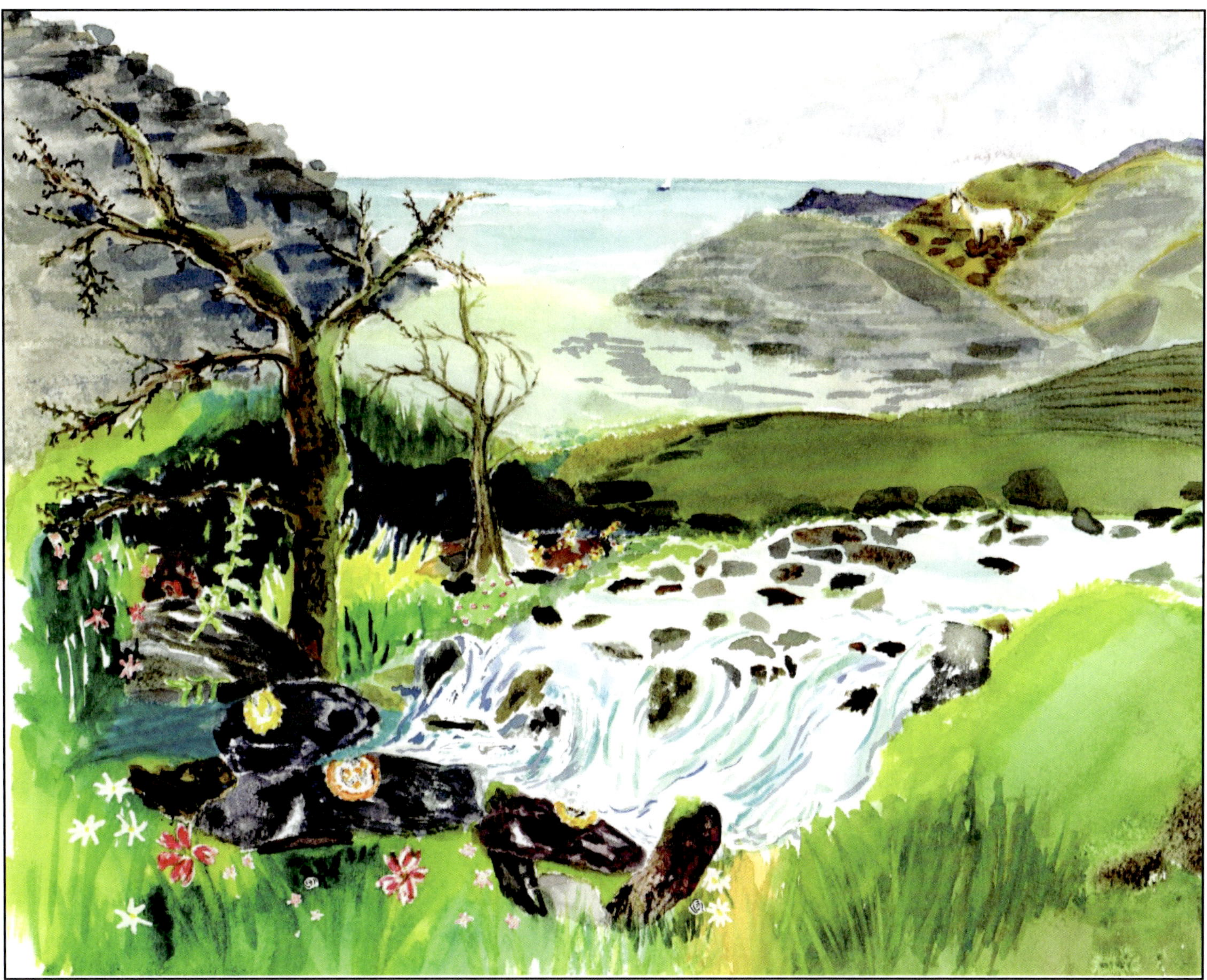

Artist's Reflection: *We spend that pretty afternoon by the Caher River. I am sitting on a tarp among the rocks, grasses and wild flowers. Paint brush poised, I'm attending, getting acquainted, breathing slowly. There are stories to tell here; secrets to reveal, whispers hanging on every note of this river's song. Oh my, there are rocks just everywhere! How do I paint these blue-black masses? Life is all around though, and I'll tell this Burren story with color. I'll use colors for liveliness, for memory, for stony beauty.*

On High, Golden Hooves and Flowing Tail

The great white horse
  of golden hooves and flowing tail,
Aonbhar once ran over the seas
  carrying a young Celtic goddess.

His progeny remain on land,
  some on the rocky edges of high Burren cliffs,
  on either side of the lush Caher Valley,
  tall and proud, standing guard
  above this valley
  where the Caher still carves its passage to the sea.

Saturated with Celtic spirit,
  this prodigal realm and its people
  are watched over
  by Aonbhar's golden-white horses
  on the cliffs of the Burren.

Poet's Notes: *As we drove down the Caher Valley road, we suddenly saw a white horse standing at the top edge of the valley, a cliff edge high up. I believe there are pastures up there but all we could see was the edge and the horse. We were told that cattle were taken up to those high pastures in the winter because it was warmer there! Warmer because of the profusion of heat-holding rock! The horse seemed a proud sentinel, and when I read the myth of Aonbhar, I knew the images I wanted for the poem.*

Mystical Horse

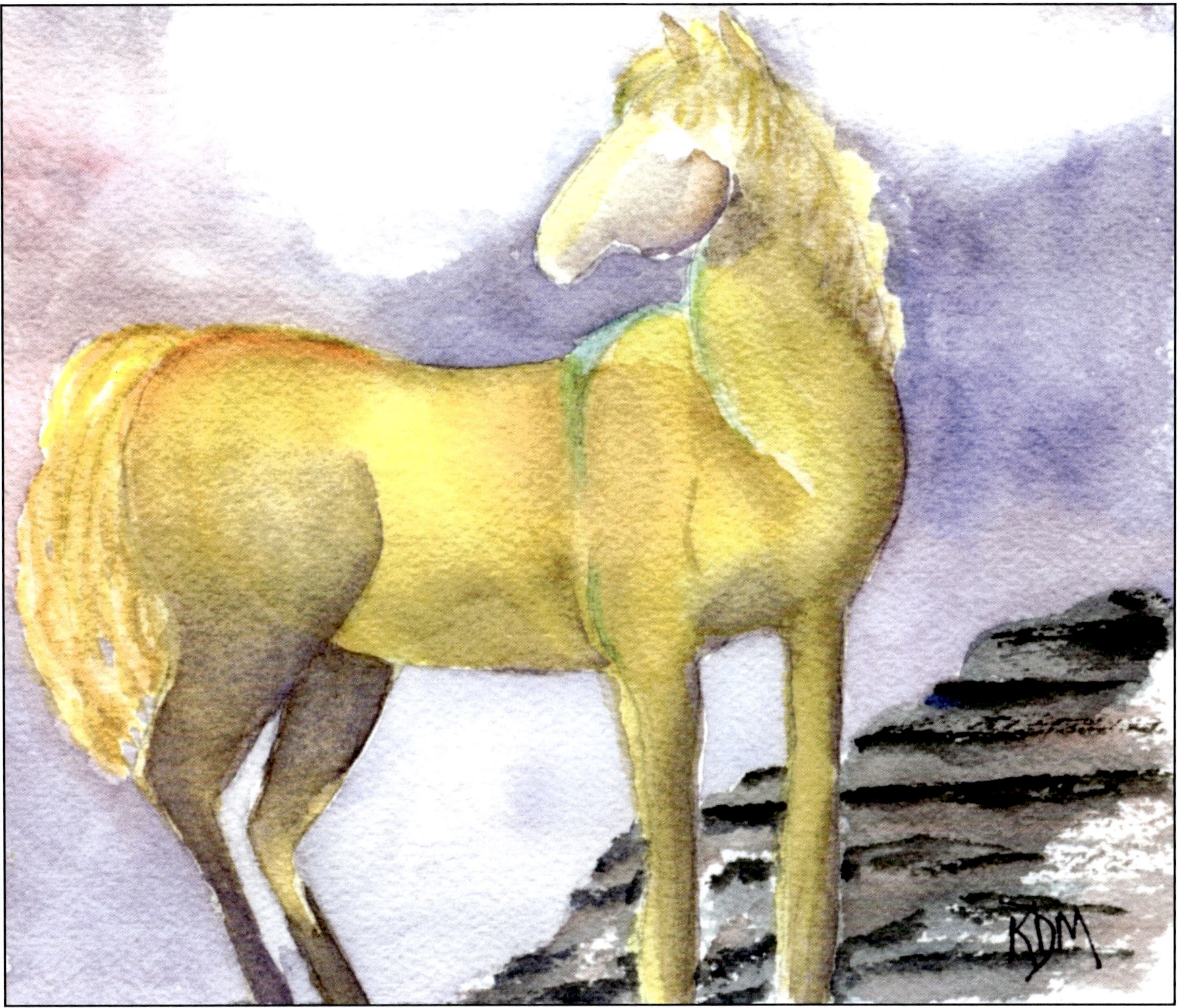

Artist's Reflection: *When I looked up and saw that creamy white horse on the cliff above, I was surprised that I wasn't surprised. He was sturdy just like a mythical horse should be. Mighty even in his quiet grass- nibbling. Great Celtic myths have horses carrying the Sun god to victory over darkness. Could I ask a blessing of this superb animal, who by now is looking directly at me? May I be as strong and steady. May I bravely carry the Light.*

Still Standing

This tree, so common in the Burren,
   seems a symbol for the tenacity of
   the people in Western Ireland.
The beautiful ocean's wind
   blows the tree in one direction only,
   and the tree survives, thrives,
   roots sunk deep in Irish soil.

In those strong winds from the Wild Atlantic,
   tree limbs flow like long tresses,
   tree's face to the winds
   daring them to blow harder.
The ocean continues its rhythmic beat.
The Caher splashes and runs down the mountain.
The only road to Fanore Beach passes the tree
   standing, chest forward, locks flowing,
   surrounded by rocks, pastures,
   challenged and changed by the elements but still standing
   strong, proud,
   a Celtic survivor.

Poet's Notes: *We saw many of these fascinating trees in the Burren, some almost pennant-like. What constant force could cause this, I wondered. The trees were quite affecting and I wanted to express their strength and determination, so like the survivor spirit of the Irish.*

Testimony

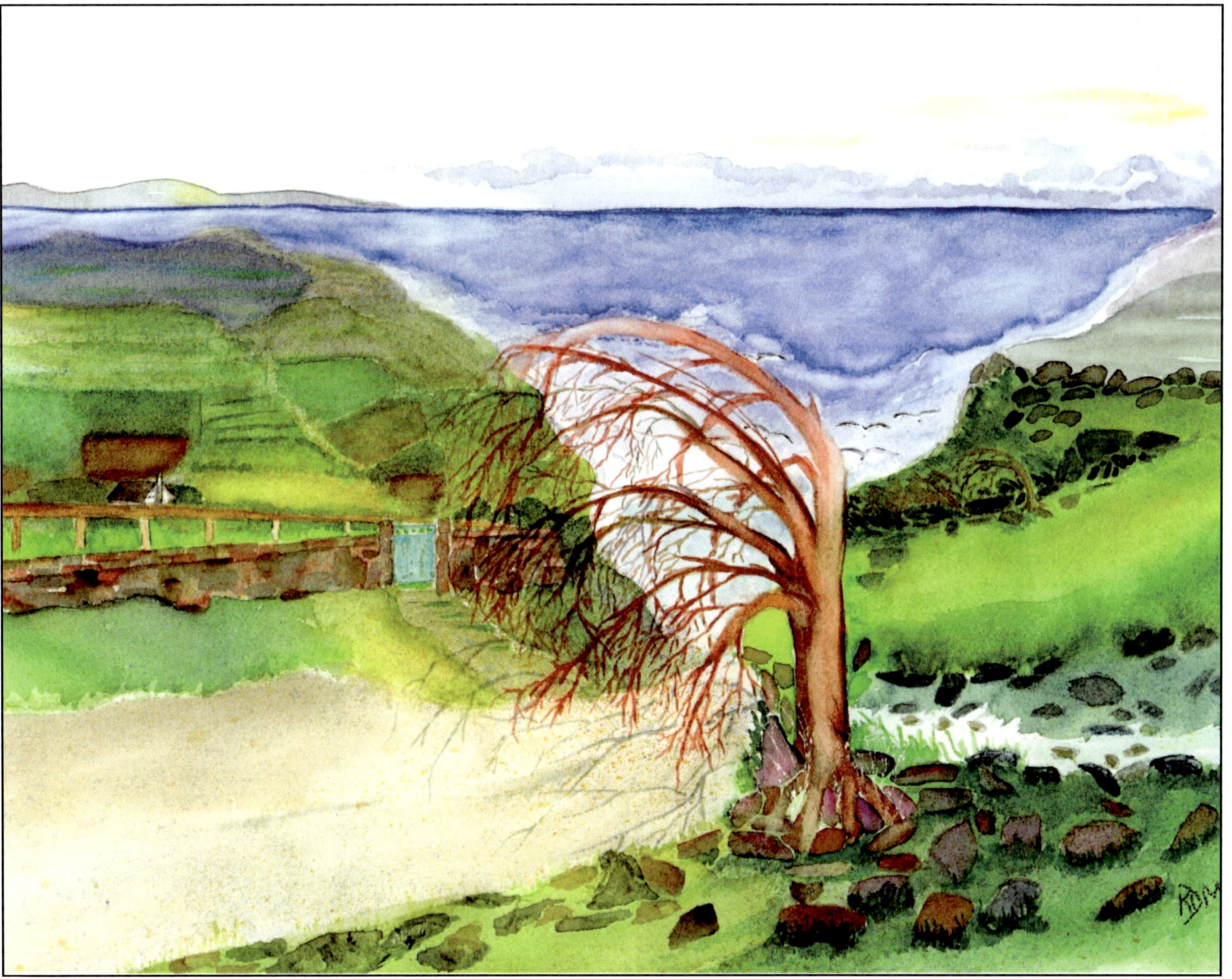

Artist's Reflection: *Wind finds its voice in the rocks, trees and crashing waves. Is this Burren tree starkly beautiful? Badly bent but alive, exposed but still offering a sort of shelter, it has adapted to a life of rough weather. Gradually, gradually, it's a vision that could transform-if we just paused. Does it mourn the loss of its expected profile? If hope, or persistence, had a shape would this tree be it?*

Leaving Home

St. Columba, in his currach,
  pushed out to sea, not for fish
  but for exile.

How brave, Columba,
  on your forced pilgrimage–
  because you copied a cherished
    psalm?

That voyage was not the Red
  Martyrdom of blood and death,
  but
  Green Martyrdom, leaving your
  beloved homeland
    for lonely rocky Iona.

And you greened! You thrived!
How you spread your faith and
    practice!
Your words and example
  still echo today through
  the lands of your influence.

Think of white birds, Celtic symbols
  of the soul. Your soul and
  your disciples' returning and
  returning as white birds,
  guides for living and reminders
  for our currach pilgrimage
    over the horizon.

Poet's Notes: *Dr. James Flannery told Kathy and me that white birds are symbols for the soul. I combined that with the idea of St. Columba crossing to Iona with his 12 companions in exile in the 7th century in a currach – a roundish hide-covered boat. I am drawn to the horizon as a life threshold and think of the white birds as souls returning as guides.*

Of Boats and Birds

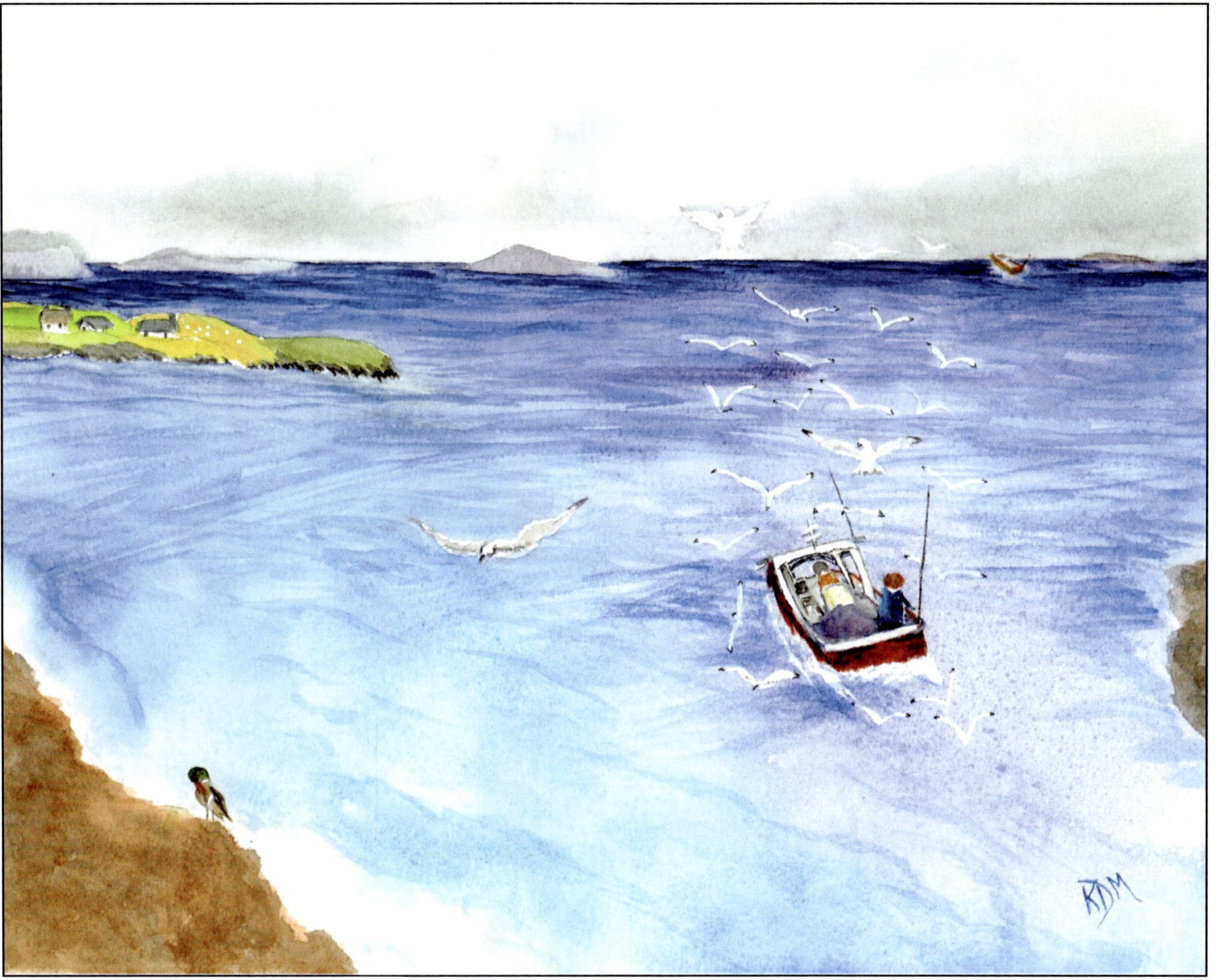

Artist's Reflection: *How brave are those souls who set out into the big ocean! They come from a long line of seekers. What are you fishing for, my dear? Are you willing to wrestle a wave or even a sea gull? I think of Brendan and Columba, Fire of Spirit loose on the water. I'm not that brave, but I do dare to search every day, in my own way.*

Contrast

sturdiness of St. Patrick's

uncontrolled ocean

contrast of energy and purpose:

sheltering church gathers, protects

ocean, overwhelms with storm

elements taken inside

elements avoided outside

    food in the sea

    a different kind in the church

Owen, his last salmon haul sold

money in his pocket, sits on the back pew

    damp, bone-weary, looks at

    the candle he lit for his long-dead wife.

He misses her still but in here somehow he is

    comforted, warmed, filled.

St. Patrick's--respite for a spirit, a filling soul-cake

Wild Atlantic--test for spirit, risk for outer life

The church, resting place for transcendence,

    faces

the ocean, life challenging master.

And there's the threshold between them

    for Owen to cross.

Poet's Notes: *The choice of color for St. Patrick's church in Fanore is arresting and though the church is nestled, facing the Atlantic, it stands out sturdily. Then, there's the Wild Atlantic, a beautiful, stormy, resource - between them, the threshold, that important Celtic concept.*

Transfiguration

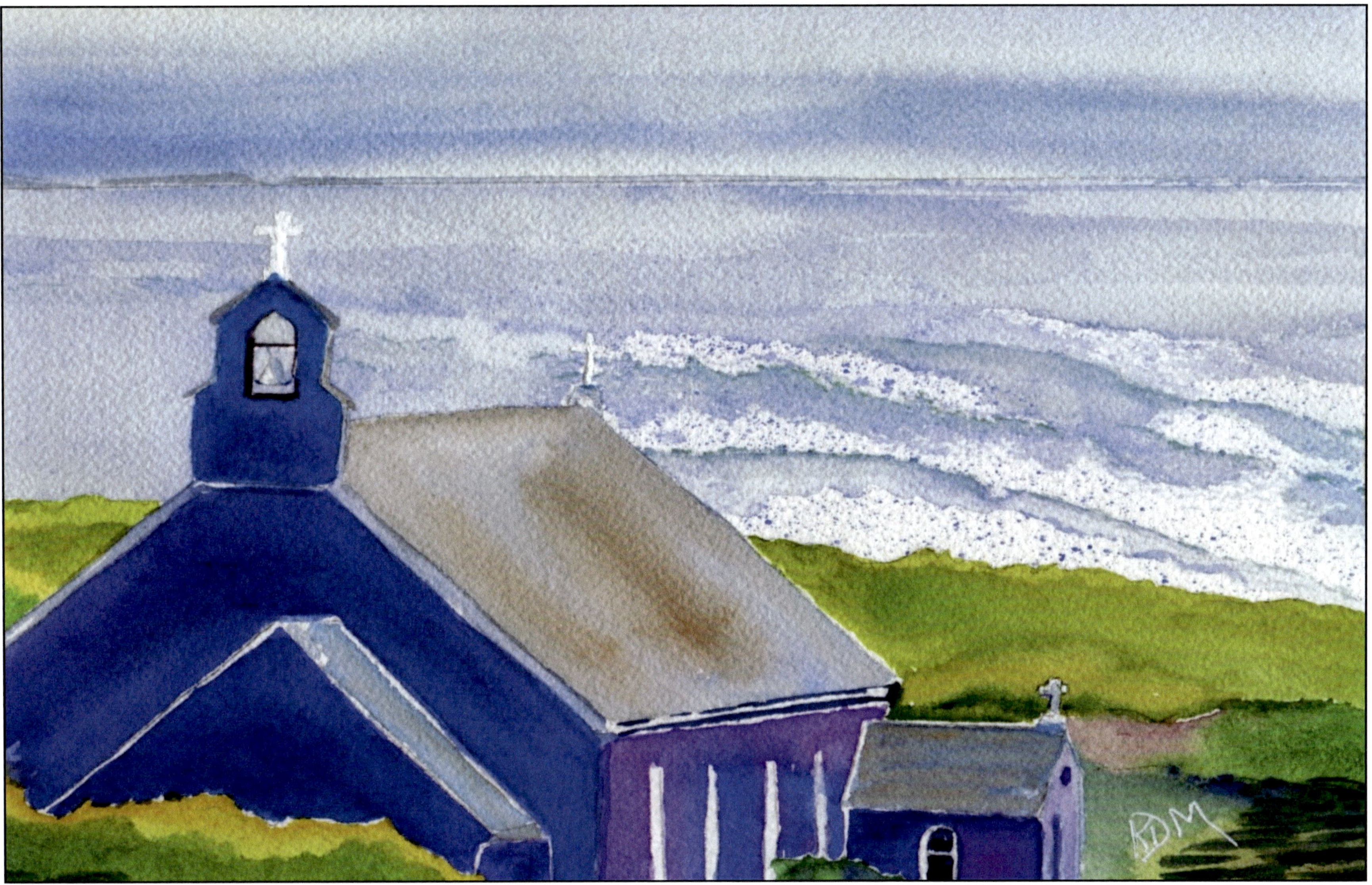

Artist's Reflection: *Yes, there it is, the small church. I was standing on the hillside above the church, next to the Caher River, looking west. From that vantage point, the small bell tower comes into focus. Its solid stone shape is filled with the tumbling ocean. In that moment I felt the power of threshold. I felt the ancient dance between stability and movement. I felt the fluid movement of transformation— a bigger view.*

The Gap of Loss

"...leaving the gap unfilled preserves the bond between us." Dietrich Bonhoeffer, *Letters and Papers from Prison*

How poignant our loss, beloveds –
you who left too early, too early.
There is a gap between
those who love you and your essence now.

This little cemetery at Craggagh
on a hill near the ocean,
not far from an ancient dolmen containing
. . . What?
Bones? Dust?
Are memories there, too?

We chant a blessing for
those lives recorded here.

And for the living left to stand, now
on the other side of the gap,
remembering, preserving
the bond between them and waiting
for the thinnest space on Samhain
to experience the beloveds again.

Poet's Notes: *In this wind-swept almost desolate place on the Wild Atlantic Way, there was a heavy sense of loss even though we knew no one buried there. I have loved Bonhoeffer's words about preserving the bond beyond death and, of course, I love the ancient Celtic belief in the nearness of the other world on October 31, the celebration of Samhain.*

Love and Respect

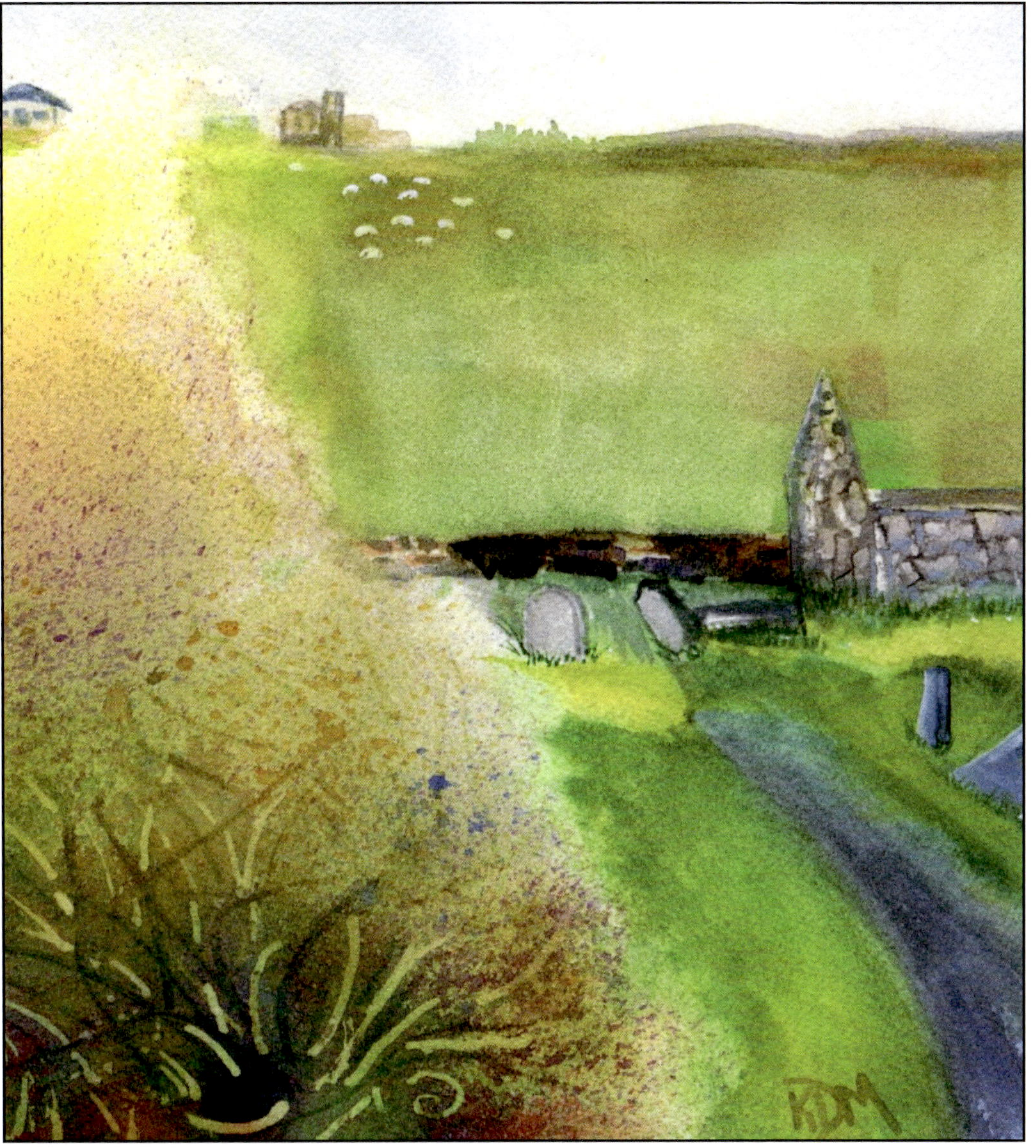

Artist's Reflection: *There is a small cemetery on the roadside in Fanore. I'm happy to return here. It's a quiet mossy place with an old stone chapel and Celtic Cross. It's a place to ponder the important questions while walking respectfully. I wonder about the people buried here, hoping for heaven, and how they loved their lives. How hard were their days? What were their hopes? Faith tells us that life and growth arise!*

Welcome

Hovered over by the threshold's angel,

Light slips out half-opened doors

   to beckon,

   to say come in

   for there is light

   inside this inner space

   and Celtic welcome

   warm, jovial, genuine.

The house stands white and clean

   thatched roof, traditional design,

Flowers, profuse in the damp fall air,

   tumble from window boxes

And the welcoming inner light invites us in.

Poet's Notes*: The first thing about this painting that struck me was the light flowing out the doors. I think this light came from Kathy's imagination and, although we had stopped at this house and admired it, I hadn't thought to write about it. White, neat homes with flowers growing so intensely were everywhere we went in Western Ireland. Kathy found something else in this scene. And, for me, the light drew me in as well as the traditionally thatched roof.*

Solace

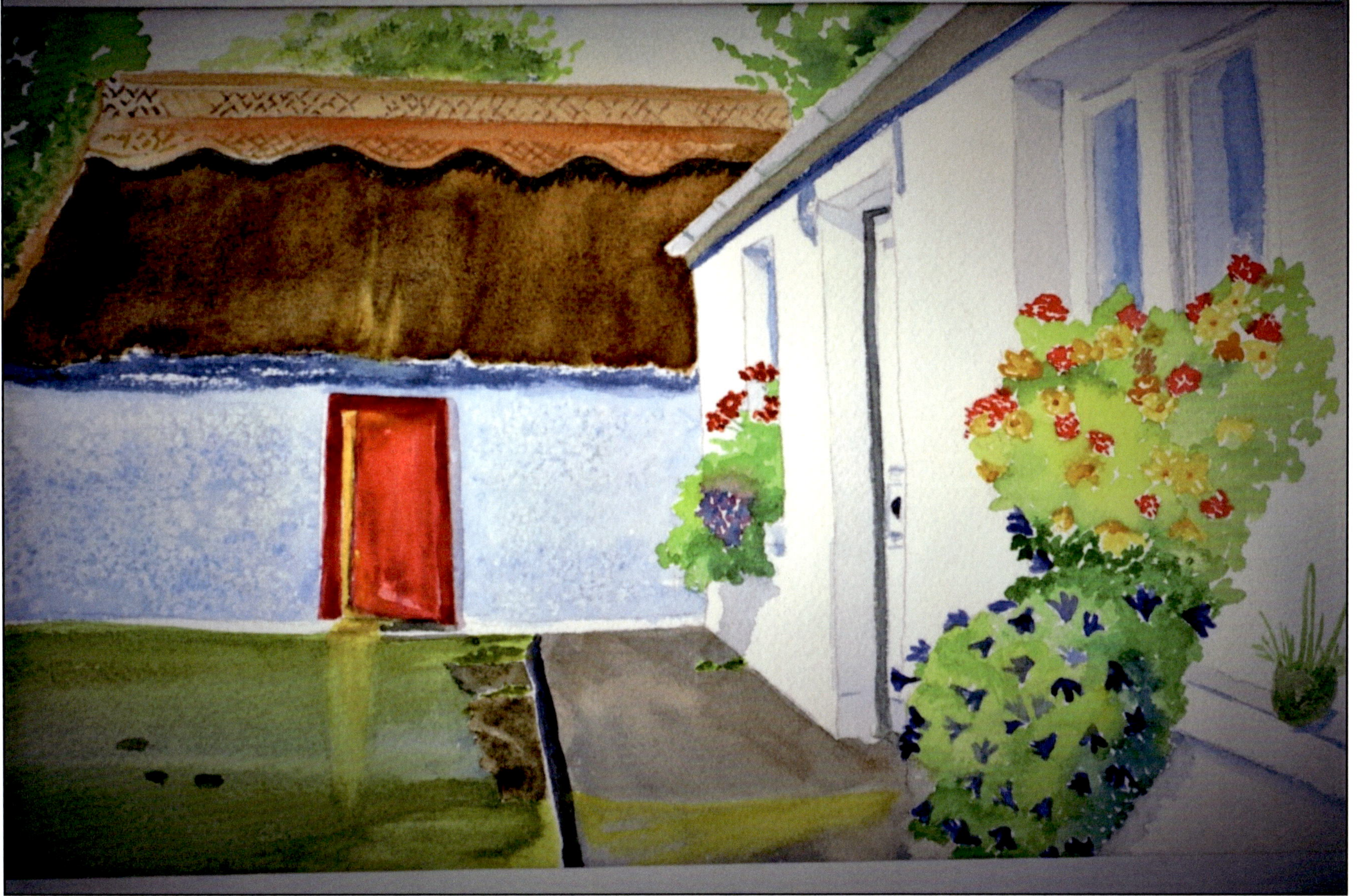

Artist's Reflection: *Clean white stone dwellings with master crafted thatched roofs are all neat and tidy. It's a real eye catcher as we drive by with those amazing flowers spilling over their containers. Are the animals that live here so well cared for? Are the people who live here so well cared for? I love the idea of growing here! Here the homes are sturdy enough to hold it all- triumph to tears- and even God, our first and forever home.*

Lough Corrib
Deep Reflective Waters

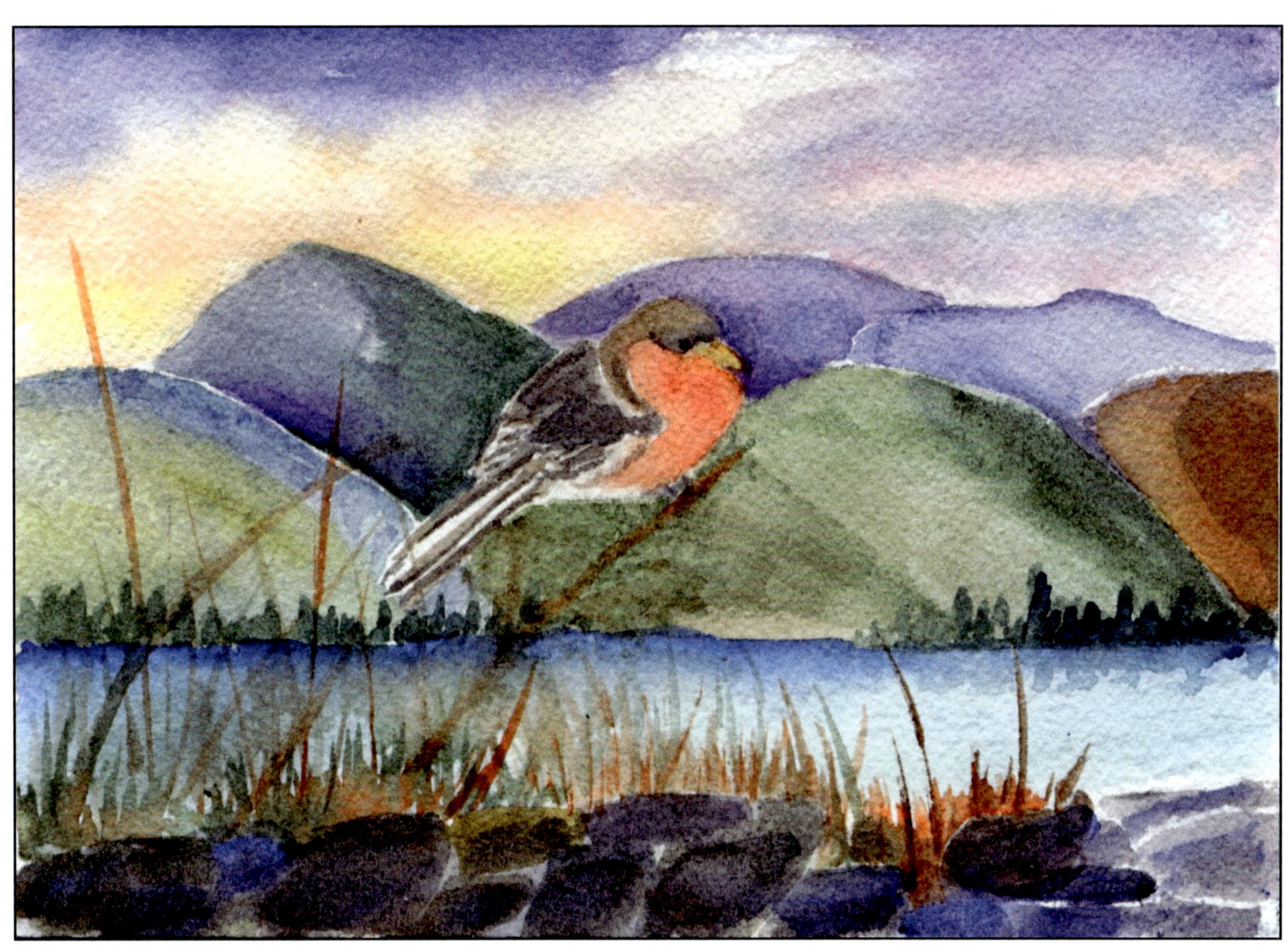

We arrive at the edge of Lough Corrib on a very dark night, grateful for the generous directions of a local family man just returning home from his work day. We are provided for once again. Lough Corrib showed her face in luminous natural and social moments.

We want to be on the eastern edge of this great lake where surprises and revelations occur. Looking west, the Connemara mountains are arched, round and ancient. Our B&B, a grand house once, with its endearing hostess, Gabriel, and a broken boiler, stands near Lough Corrib's lone lighthouse and the ruins of a Norman castle.

The raw, gray morning becomes more sullen as the hours go by, so we retreat to Ballycurrin House's great room with its big fireplace and high windows. What a welcome haven this is after exploring the shoreline and the castle ruins. Wrapping our cold fingers around steaming cups of tea, Kathy paints; Patty writes. Later, Patty leads us all in Tai Chi. Gabriel is simply delighted to learn each movement.

Our next day supplies one of the jewels of our pilgrimage. We participate in a rare gorgeous sunset. The sparkling lake is at our feet beyond the great brooding rocks at its edge while those distant, marvelous mountains turn blue and then purple. We stand in silent awe, accompanied by a small chaffinch and a munching cow.

Would we like to come to a party? Yes, of course we would. Gabriel has planned a welcome party for some new neighbors, although she is a newcomer herself. The group that gathers in the great room is friendly and curious. We are Irish, American, Dutch, South African, German and British, all living in this remote little "neighborhood."

Now it's our turn to sing a song for the group. Oh, it must be an American song, preferably one they could sing along with us. Based on the jokes and the music so far, we are a bit taken back.

Our choice?

"On top of Spaghetti" from Sesame Street, and it's a howling success with the mini UN partying on that chilly night at Ballycurrin House.

Thresholds are everywhere, and our stance is: Yes.

Lanterns and Questions

Small children are like lanterns
   throwing light on unexamined landscapes
   by continually asking why.

Their delightful questions and, sometimes,
   our beautiful adult queries,
   the ones born of wonder in the soul,
   shine in the dark of unknowing,
light the lanterns of the heart-mind,
shine on the hidden,
      tiny snails in weeds, a heart-stone in Fanore sand,
      beauty unseen, unfelt until lit,
reveal paths, vistas, understandings,
new ways of feeling, seeing,
open to beauty and
revelations at any age
with the illumination of a good question.

Poet's Notes*: I love the young child's mind – so open and with no cultural filter. It seems to me that most seekers (pilgrims) love a good question. And I thought of both as shining light for understanding.*

Lantern Light

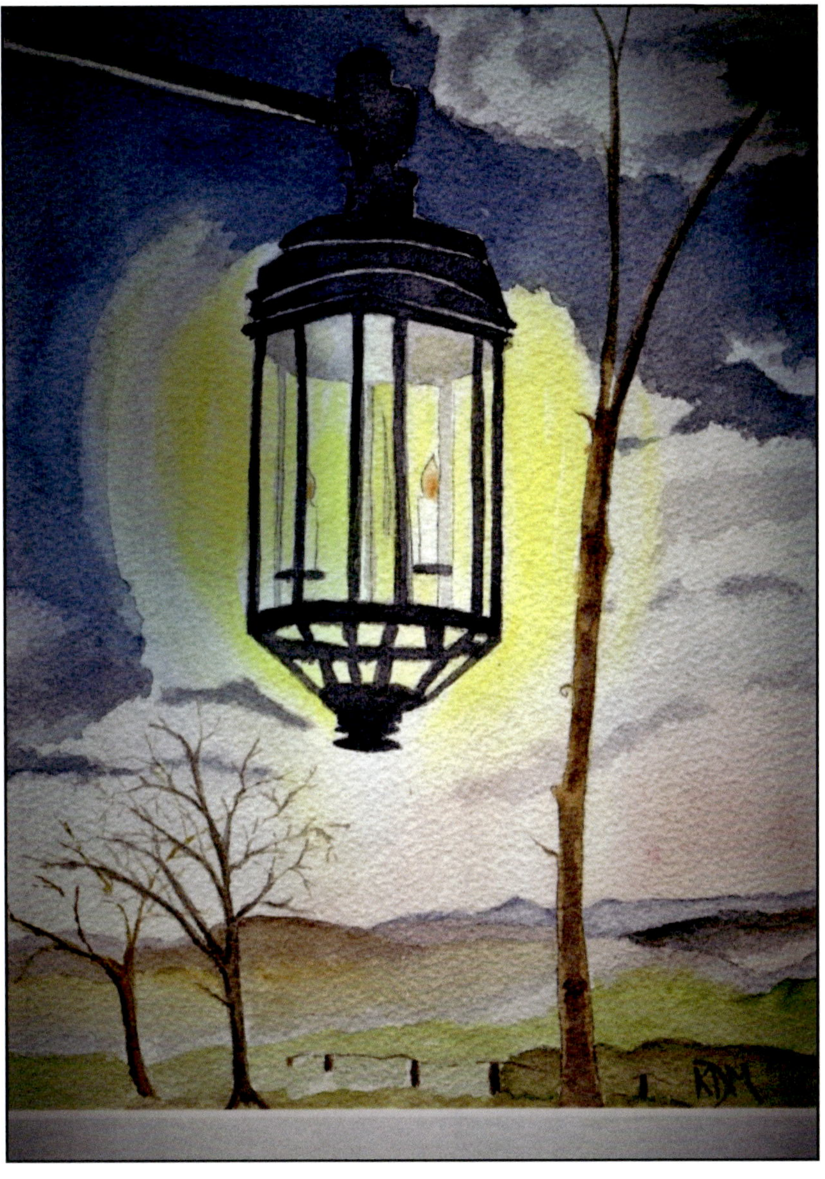

Artist's Reflection: *Lantern Light helps me see; helps me find my way in the dark. Imagination grabs the wild edges of light and runs toward the mountains of challenge. This pilgrimage is about seeing differently. It's about surrendering to whatever lights and invites illumination. It's about daring to explore inner and outer landscapes during liminal hours, trusting that there will be enough light to see what I need to see.*

Witness and Sentinel

The lighthouse on Lough Corrib
    stands as a sentinel
    guarding the boaters on the loch.

It is witness
    to fierce storms
    which whip waters,
    fishermen in their boats.

And is witness to
    the lough's complete calm
    hiding the life beneath the surface.

The lighthouse, strong and silent,
    may also have the Celtic gift
      of deep witnessing to feel and
    hear from the depths
    the lough's
    still
      magic
      music.

Poet's Notes: *What a wonder and surprise to find a small lighthouse on a rocky point on Lough Corrib near where we stayed at Ballycurrin House. It attests to both the size of the lough and its turbulence. Deep witnessing is the translation of the Celtic word, Teannalach.*

Shelter of Light

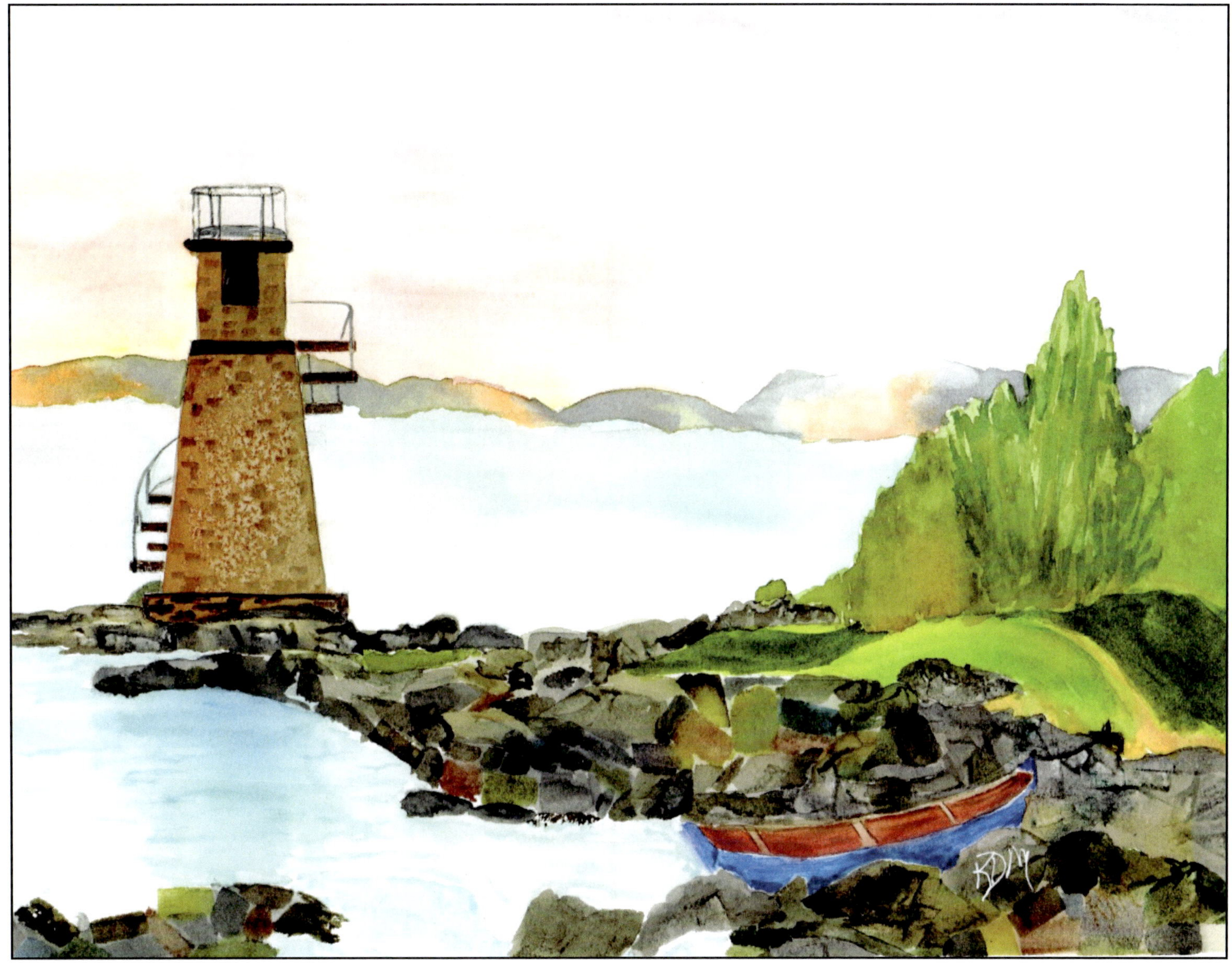

Artist's Reflection: *Surprise! There's a lighthouse on the eastern shore of Lough Corrib right near Ballycurrin House. The day is becoming more raw and windy by the minute. Charmed by the blue boats and sturdy stone lighthouse, I imagine more than one sailor/pilgrim was blessed to see its beam of light coming through the storm or fog. A blessing and a warning- can it be both? There are rocks here, pay attention, it's risky! The safe harbor is worth it.*

Essence of a Lough

At the whim of cloud, wind, sun,
   Lough Corrib changes personality,
   her surface roiled with storms
   or absolutely glassy blue in absence of wind.

We know her surface personality,
   but her essence?
In the depths and shallows there must be life:
   slithering grasses and creatures,
   fish avoiding anglers' hooks
   then growing to prize-winning size.
Still, we land creatures, do we
   really know the lough?

The surface is the threshold
   and we, on one side
   of the silvery blue or turgid green door,
   are dreaming the depths,
   loch monsters, eel grasses
   skin-shedding Roane, shape-shifting kelpies –
   and the true watery essence of the lough.

Poet's Notes: *Imagining a wild sort of aquatic life, in a water world below, I also added Celtic mythological beings in the depths of Lough Corrib because it made me smile. Since I imagine fairies in the woods, why not mythical creatures in the lough's depths?*

Teannalach

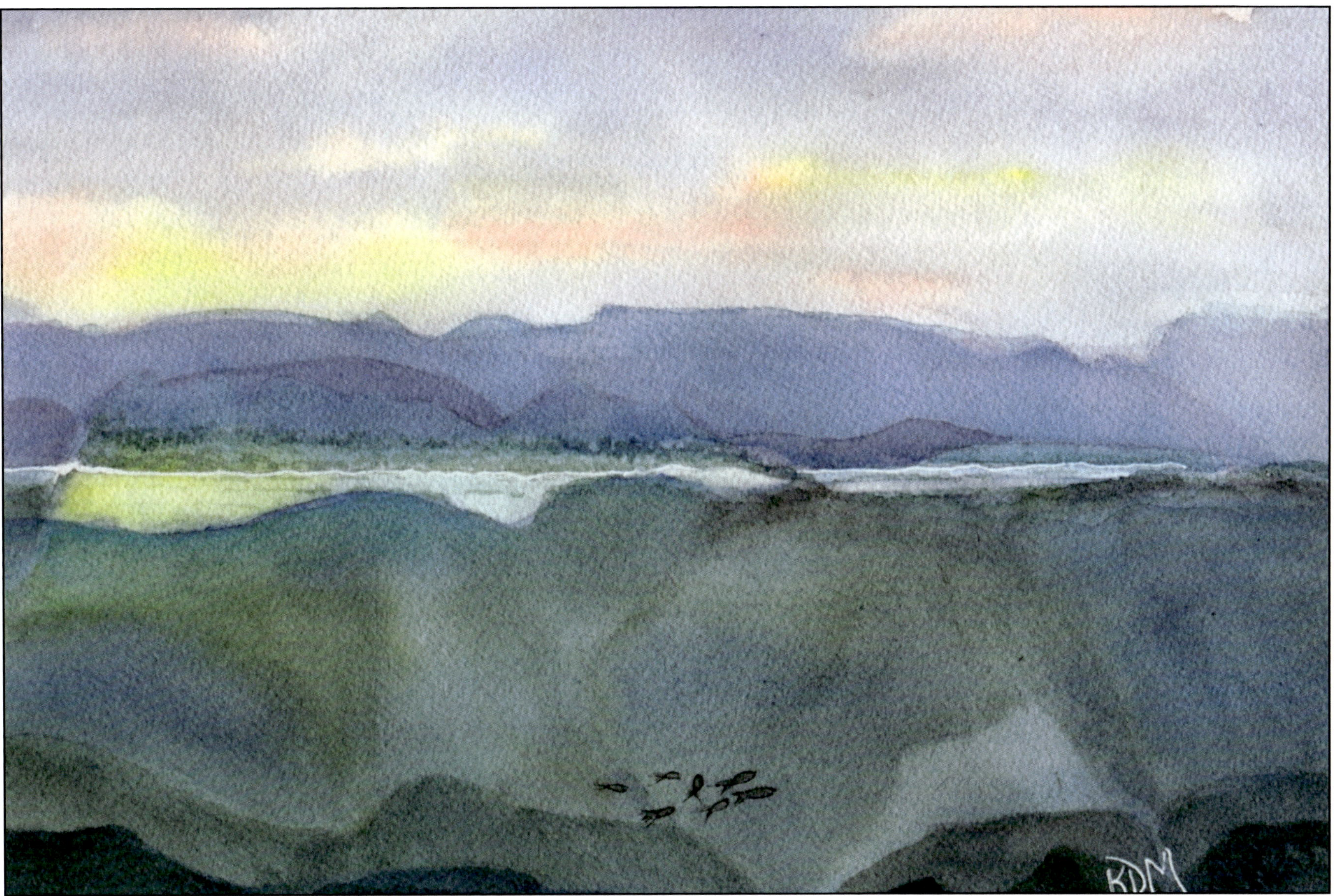

Artist's Reflection: *What, I wondered, is below the surface of Lough Corrib? What is that landscape like? Mountains, hidden, unseen for thousands of years, except by fish and deep diving cormorants? Light and shadow? Mountains and gullies? Music too? Waiting for the moment of discovery, there is mountain music- above and below so listen with the ears of your heart.*

Blue Rest

Blue boats rest, waiting for the next trip

   into choppy waters or better,

   glassed blue-sky water

   when a partly cloudy sky

   turns all the earth a subtle blue,

   a transfiguration of water, trees, boats

   all the Connemara mountains.

Lough Corrib becomes a momentary scene

   of incomparable blue and peace.

Poet's Notes: My husband and I stayed on Lough Corrib, the western shore, near Oughterard in Sept. 2015. I was so disappointed at the view – the lake barely visible because of the low site of the B&B and the reedy shore. We drove on a scenic route to try to find a view that would include the Connemara mountains but with no luck. Kathy and I looked for a place on the eastern shore. Our stay in Ballycurrin House gave us the views I wanted.

Little Blue Boats

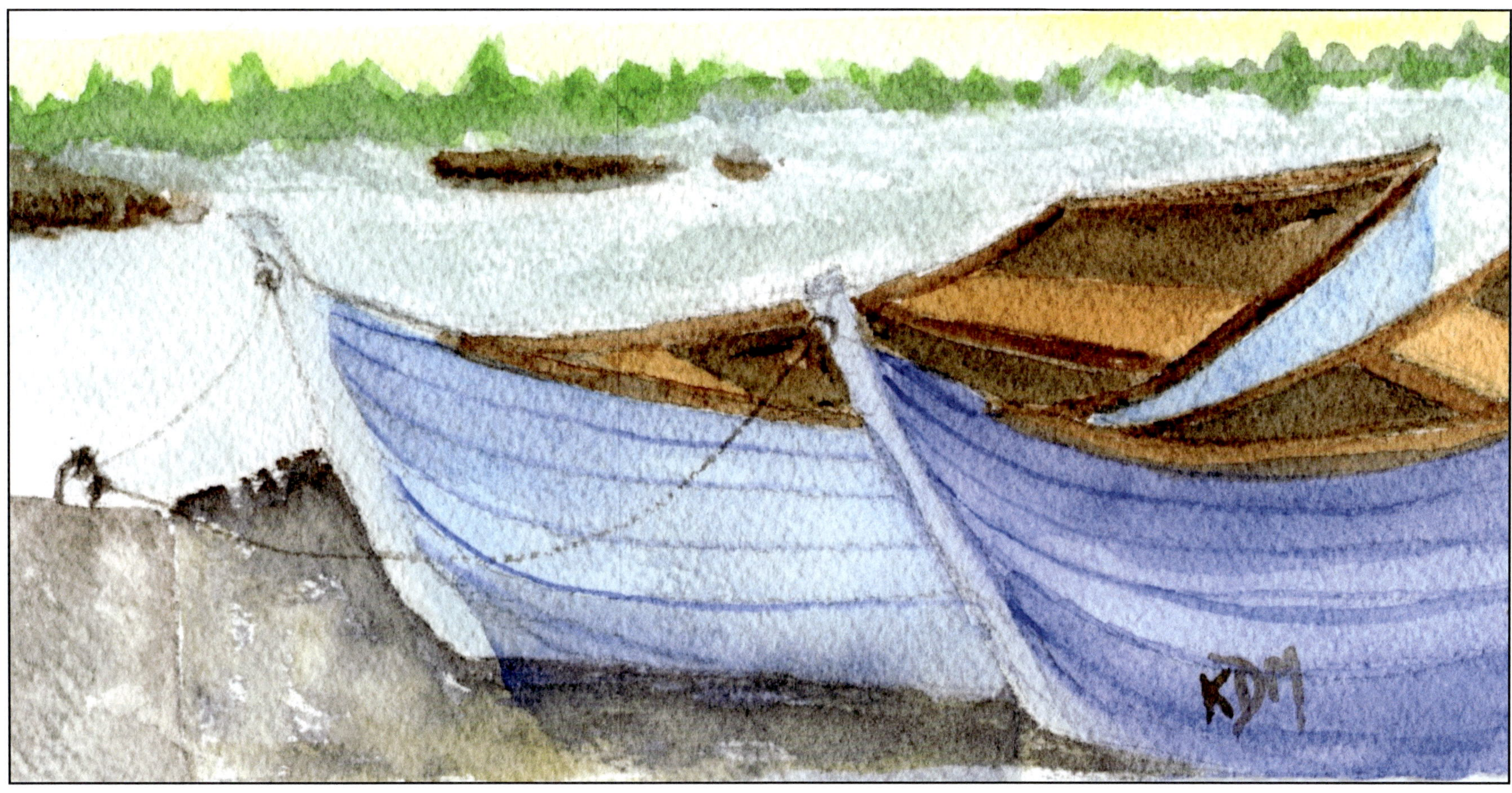

Artist's Reflection: *Descendants of Brendan's currach, Lough Corrib's boats are chunky, little and bright blue. No doubt they are designed for this lake. I bet they're good at their job. Boats mean possibility. Today is windy and raw through and through. No boats are out on the lake. So here they sit, lined up on the edge almost like the first creatures that crawled from water to land.*

Watch?

Why not watch the western light,

  the sun transfiguring the world,

  from daily dull to shimmering

  in colors too intense to copy?

One last brilliant display

  over and through the Connemara Mountains

  changing pale blue clouds

  to darkest blue with fissures

  of colors so unnatural to the sky-

  tangerine, sherbet orange, lavender-

  that they seem of another realm?

This light display lifts my heart skyward

  from the dulling shore

  to the immensely beautiful sky world.

Standing on this threshold, a realm all its own,

  I fall in love all over again

  with sky, color, cloud movements

  and the gift of liminal space.

Poet's Notes: The hour that Kathy and I spent standing on the eastern shore of Lough Corrib was like an enchantment. The sun and clouds danced to a magic choreography. Who could have designed, planned this astonishing sight? The sense of place under the Western Irish sky was strong. We only left because the light was diminishing, and we were standing on small rocks. Turning to go, we heard a snort. Less than ten feet away was a large cow (a fence between her and us). That grounded us! Perhaps she was simply guarding us in the growing dusk.

In the Company of Sunset on Lough Corrib

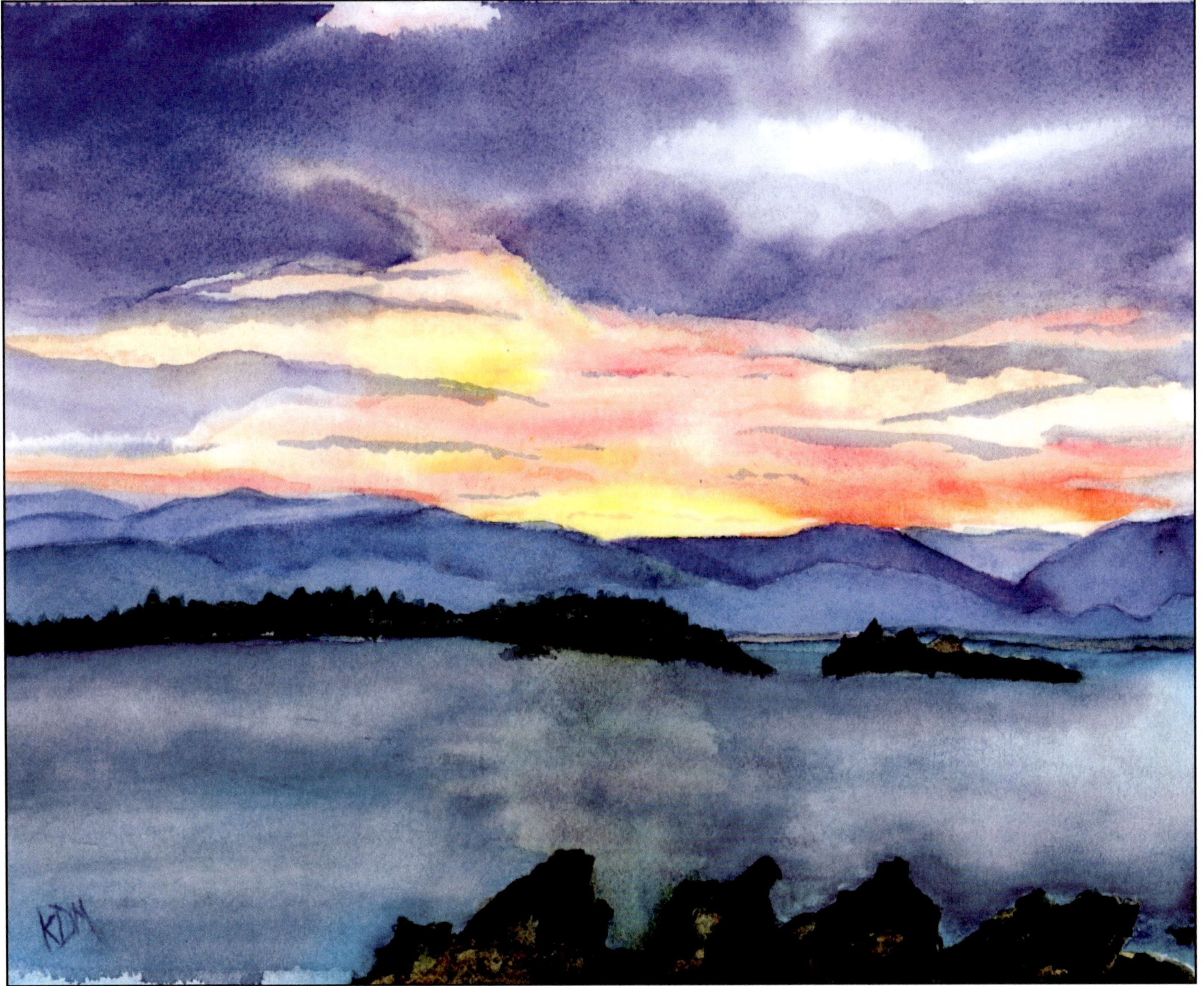

Artist's Reflection: *How often do you get such a sunset on Lough Corrib? Stop In Your Tracks! Watch! Notice the glorious, lingering departure of day. We can know the character of the Creator in these thresholds if we pay attention. Like calls to like. The part of the Creator that's embedded in me gets activated in a deep way at such glorious moments as these and I wonder if anything is impossible.*

Regenerating

Life's peregrination
 spirals up and out
  from a singular point of energy
   growing wider and farther

The soul's window opens to the source point
 of energy, wonder, creativity
 spiraling in and out.

The Celts journeyed, wandered,
 left home to find a sacred well,
 found a monastery, sing poetry, teach
 with that innate push to go wandering,
  leaving, learning,
  finding the inner still point
  and winding out again like
  curled millipedes,
   fern fronds, fractals, galaxies.
  Spirals.
   Spirals.
    Life.

Poet's Notes: *The kernel of this poem did not come easily. How to write about a spiral in an eye? Even Kathy's well-thought out ideas didn't speak to or approach me. Then I saw a book of mine on mandalas, looked at the section on spirals and realized what I needed to write about – the ubiquity and importance of the spiral everywhere and especially to the Celts.*

Looking and Seeing

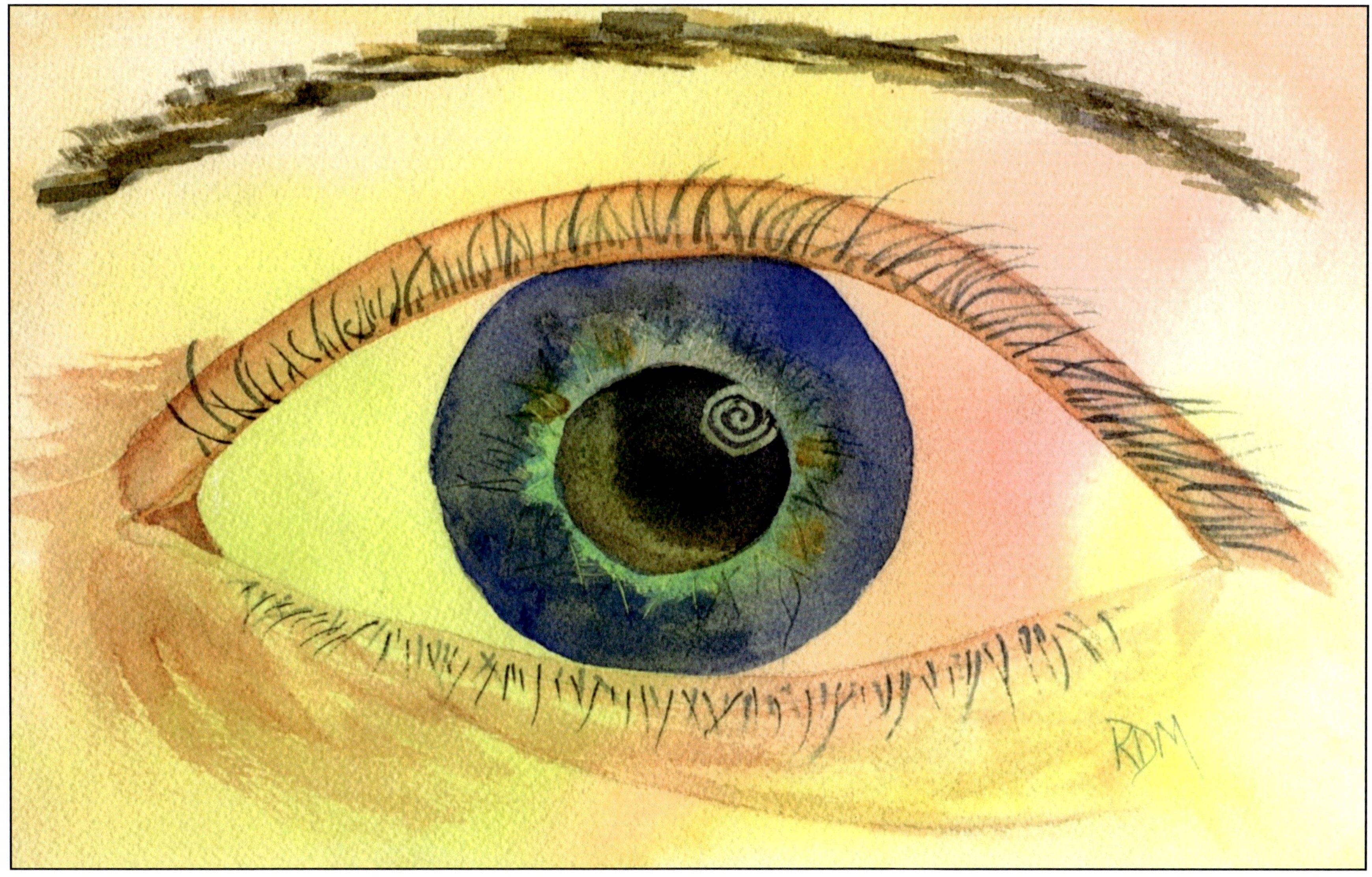

Artist's Reflection: *Who sees their familiar landscape with new eyes every day? What colors are absorbed? What colors are rejected? (Mollica, Color Theory, pg 8-9) What a funny thing has happened. I notice that I am much more present to what's all around me. I notice the red bricks and think, "Wow, blue and yellow are absorbed and are in there somehow, somewhere." Who stands in the gap- that rugged, fertile terrain? Whose vision helps me see?*

The Invitation

"The starting place is a sense of wonder."
Mary Catherine Bateson

One step to the open gate
   moving toward a little journey,
   a wander through to the other side filled
   with the unknown and wonder:

Perhaps an odd-shaped red stone,
  or an ancient giant of a tree
    hovering over the path,
  a black and white magpie swooping
    over the shore of Lough Corrib,

A crumbled Norman castle, partly standing
  or the wonder of another human
  and a conversation that wanders
  into your own unknown territory
  to bless you with a new landscape
    opening within you,

All because you accepted
  the invitation of the open gate.

Poet's Notes: *The open gate invited me to wander and so I did while we stayed at Ballycurrin House. Having done the Camino de Santiago at a slow pace, a wandering pace, I used that tempo for discovery both in the Burren and here at Lough Corrib. I think I wandered in a state of wonder and that I was joy-filled. Much later I heard Dr. Bateson interviewed; her phrase summed up my perspective on this trip.*

I'm Open

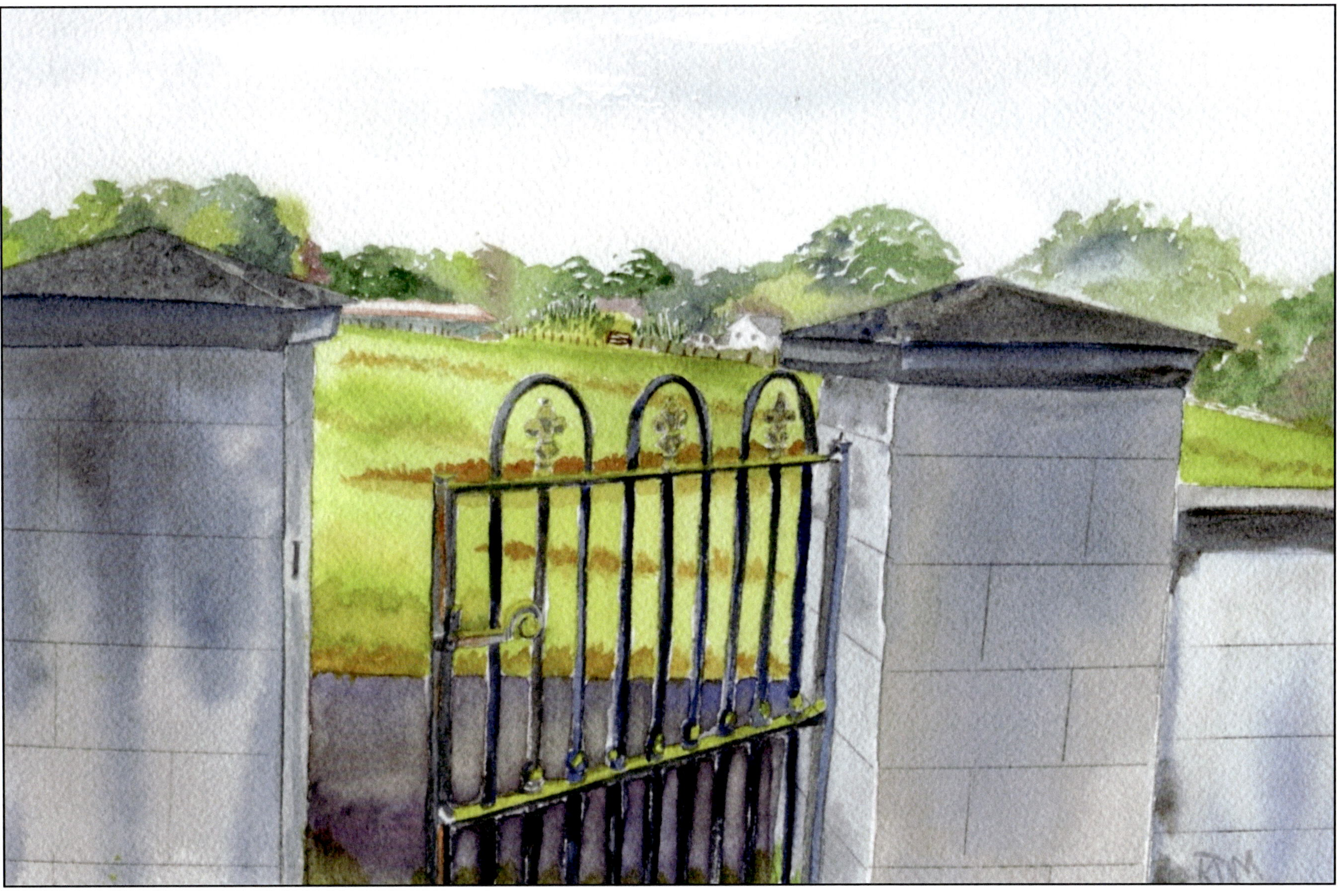

Artist's Reflection: *Pausing on the top step as I enter Ballycurrin House, I notice another threshold. The gate has swung open. The wall isn't the only limit. There are spaces around and in between. That's where wisdom lives…and adventure*

Table, Waiting at Ballycurrin House

Empty chairs, empty table,
  empty space
      that waits to be filled with words from
      two beings who ask respond query
      listening, not planning the response,
      deep cellular listening
  where change happens.

What questions will there be? What stories?
Humor? Pathos?

There is a space waiting here
  for the energy of ideas and change,
  words falling like acid or balm
  on the heart-mind.

This table and these chairs are ready
  holding the space, the threshold,
  neither the heavens nor the earth
But the space in between
  where the miraculous can happen.

Poet's Notes: *The art of conversation, the deep exchange, was so important to Celtic mystics. That's what I thought of when I saw this empty social space in the side yard of Ballycurrin House. The small table and chairs looked rather lonely. It was too cold for me to sit outside. The set captured Kathy's artistic attention and, as I took in her painting, it made me think of conversations to be held.*

Two Chairs - One Conversation

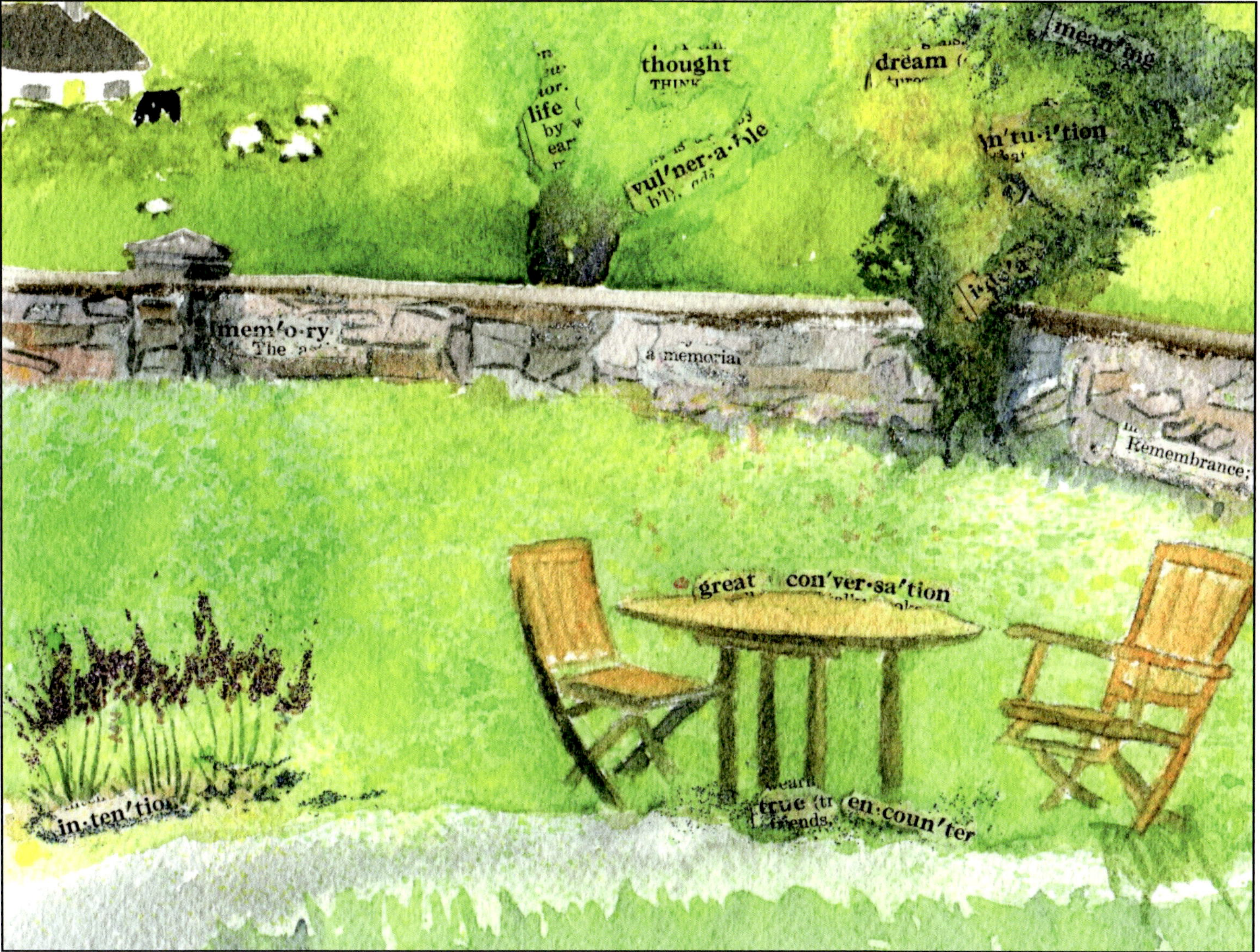

Artist's Reflection: *Oh, the grass was so green as I looked over at the terrace ringed with an ancient stone wall. What would it be like to sit there having a conversation? Settled in our chairs, with drinks on the table, I feel shy. There is no rush. There is truth spoken here. When was the last time that deeply shared time invited you to sparkle like that very green Irish grass?*

Mandala and Trap

The garden spider working out her life's purpose
  creates a mandala from her own body,
  intricate, large.

She is purposeful, dogged in her task.
Did she think to make a cocoon
  and metamorphose?
 Did she wish to weave a lovely silken dress for herself?

No. She created a complicated skirt.
All spokes of this skirt-web
  lead to the center, to her.

We marvel at her mandala
  so practical, so beautiful.

Her creation summons our imagination
  to contemplate the real and bring forth
  truths from deep within.
So we have a utilitarian spider web for catching food
  and a beautiful mandala for our imagination
  and for our deep longing for a web of connection.

Poet's Notes: *This huge spider web was an impressive work of art – most are! I did think of the shape as a mandala but for the spider it is a trap for food. So, we have both the practical and the symbolic, then the important part – the center.*

Web of Belonging

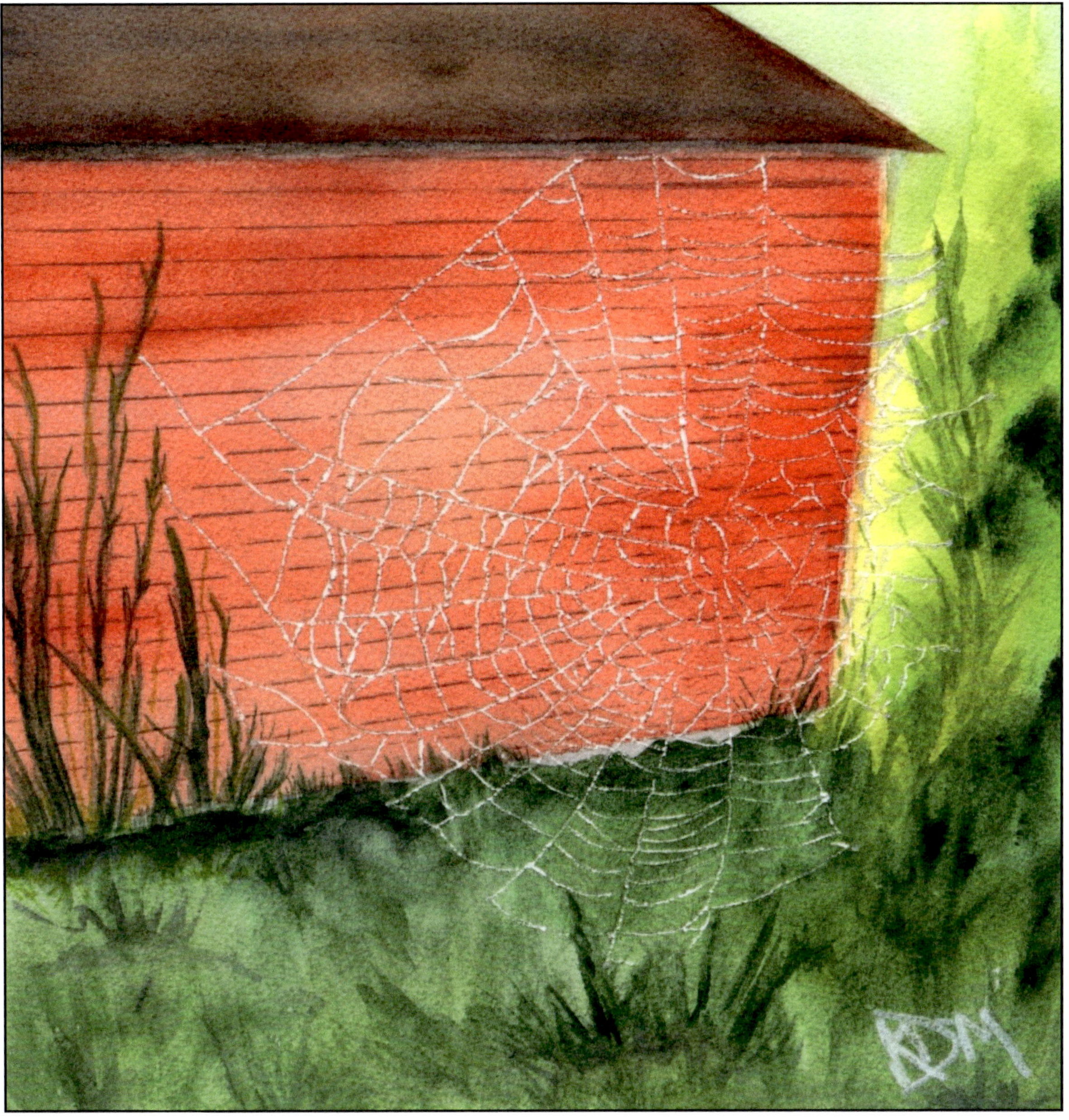

Artist's Reflection: *This beautiful spider web was shimmering with dew against a red shed. I spied it there in the weeds while I filled the car with gas. Connections are everywhere if only we could see them. People, plants and yes, animals are all growing, expanding together or not at all on this planet. The truth is that we learn so much in the spaces within life's webbing. Nature mimics spirit.*

Connemara

High Spaces Thin Places

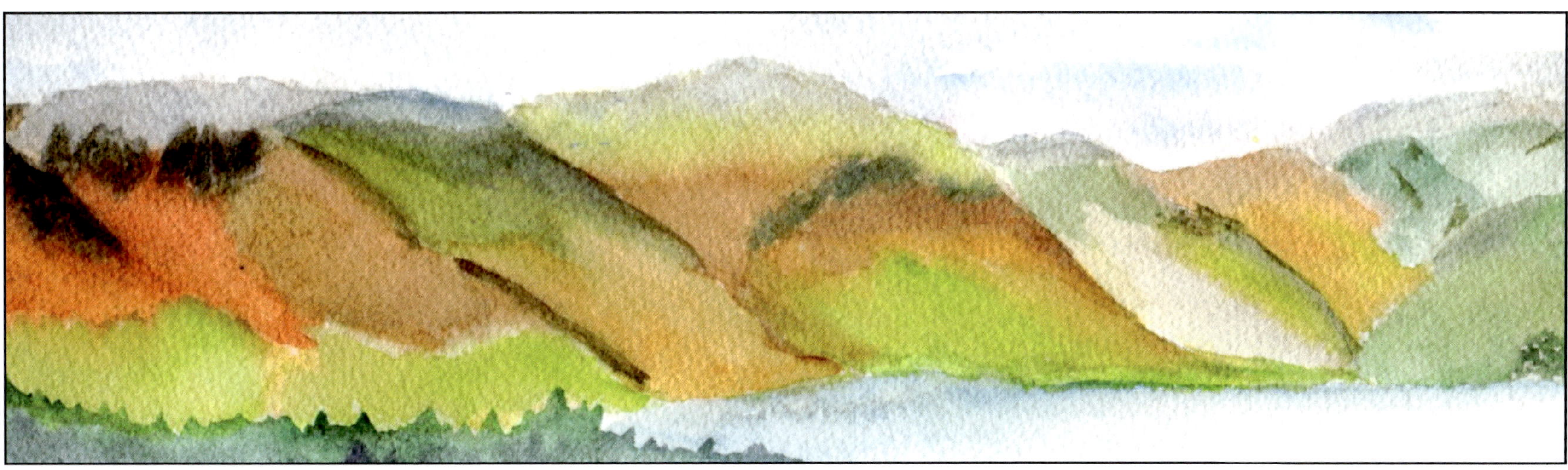

"I am anxious!" says Kathy. The directions to our next B&B describe mountainous ridges and amazing views. Driving on a narrow mountain road -- on the left. Yikes!

One step at a time, we remind ourselves. This is a pilgrimage after all. Courage enough will be provided, and hopefully, continued protection.

Arriving in this rough ancient land of bogs and lakes, it seems the Ice Age receded just weeks ago. Mountains here are rounded, covered in carelessly thrown rugs of green and rusty grasses. If we are seeking beauty, then Route 344 should be named the beautiful, mostly flat, straight road. The moody mountains are glorious! Beside us are golden fields and shaggy sheep who call this road their own. Not another soul is nearby on this sunny, crisp day. We are sheltered by floating clouds and ancient mountains. Our senses are awakened more deeply by the shapes and colors of Connemara in late fall.

It's worth noting how one synchronicity can lead to another unexpected possibility. Weeks before our pilgrimage, Kathy had *happened* upon a David Whyte poem. It mentioned a place called Mamean. She followed the breadcrumb trail. It led to a 2009 article in the *Irish Independent* newspaper by Christopher Somerville. The article describes the renewal of an ancient pilgrimage route, a passage between mountains where, historically, the local people gathered for Mass, hidden away from persecuting British soldiers. Before that, Mamean was a pre-Christian holy place of worship and exchange. Meanwhile, Patty discovered Mamean in John Quinn's lovely book, *Walking on the Pastures of Wonder*. Hiking the ancient Mamean Pilgrimage Path becomes the focal point of our time in Connemara. How we will find the Path is the big question. All we have is the hand drawn map copied from the old newspaper article.

The day is crisp and windy. Amazingly, we find the tiny road leading to the Mamean Pilgrimage Path! The Path itself is impressively steep and very rocky. Here is another time for us to take a deep breath, and just take the first step. Remember courage is available.

Our intention is continued openness to receive whatever gift of insight or conversation is presented to us. Immediately upon opening the car trunk to get our gear, we are approached by a spritely older man. It is Father Paddy. Introducing himself and his friend Barbara, he tells us how they have just walked five miles. He is 84 years old.

"Would we walk awhile with the girls?" Father Paddy asks Barbara as we pull on our wind pants and hiking boots. "Yes of course. After all, it is Mamean," she agrees. So off we all go, and he leaves us in the dust!

Father Paddy is waiting for us as we puff up to the crest with its granite statue of St Patrick. He asks if we think he looks like St Patrick, kidding that he had been the model. He actually does look like the statue. After filling bottles with holy well water, he pronounces a blessing for us (Prayer of St Patrick) and then breaks into song. Patty, who sings beautifully, joins in, and finally Barbara and Kathy do too. There we four stand. We have a clear view to the Atlantic over mountains, bogs and lakes. The wind is whistling. Our voices are lifted in a blessed song. This still is a moment to treasure.

Later, we sit in the cover of the tiny chapel, near St Patrick's bed, a cove in the stone. We are silent as we meditatively eat our sandwiches, sketch and write.

On our way back down the Path, we chat with a couple of "hillwalkers." There are so many stories.

As we drive toward Renvyle House the next day, we decide to visit Killary Fjord and the town of Leenane with its icy cobalt water, fishing farms, and faery trees. Later that afternoon Connemara National Park beckons us. The lovely park hosts a Poets' Walk, a fine mountain hike as well as a very informative exhibit on bogs and peat.

Kathy recommended Renvyle House because she had been there before and knows there is a lovely conservatory full of light and red geraniums. It would be a perfect place to recollect. Our hope is to begin to pull all the threads of our experiences together. How will we weave these adventures? Patty has not written the poems she expected to write. Kathy has only been able to paint reference sketches *en plein air*. Our days have been unusually sunny, but chilly.

 Another synchronicity awaits us. Our room, 54, overlooks Killary Fjord, mountains, local homes and of course, shaggy sheep. We open the door and gasp at the beautiful view and our good fortune. Awaking early the next morning, we part the heavy curtains. There is the crescent moon lingering as the first yellows of sunrise appear. We remember the Celtic invitation to pause and notice. Beauty and wisdom are found in ordinary daily happenings.

Like Celtic knot work, attending to the particular while being open to the greater threads of life, we weave a memorable pattern in lives lived beautifully.

Road 344

Grasses stoutly wave in autumnal winds,
  do not fall or break but
  wait for grazing sheep to cut them down.

Rich grass green fields, now dying
  and gone to saffron-color,
  hug Road 344 cutting through Connemara.

Mountains on either side hold the land in place
  as the road goes on and has no end, but heads toward
  purple, gray, brown massive bens.

Perhaps there is an ending, an Omega point
  here, grass sheep roads mountains merge
  into some great infinity,
  the complex Connemara light carrying all this,
  to an unseen vanishing point full of
  beauty, love, spirit.

Poet's Note: *There is such distance to the north-northwest heading along this road, Road 344, that looked to have no end, no horizon. The grass had turned ochre yellow, and a few sheep wandered the road, grazing, oblivious to any traffic – well, there wasn't any really! The landscape had no human input except a fence here and there and the paved road. I was taken by the sense of infinity in the distance and being funneled in that direction. I thought of Teilhard de Chardin and his Omega Point.*

The Road Through

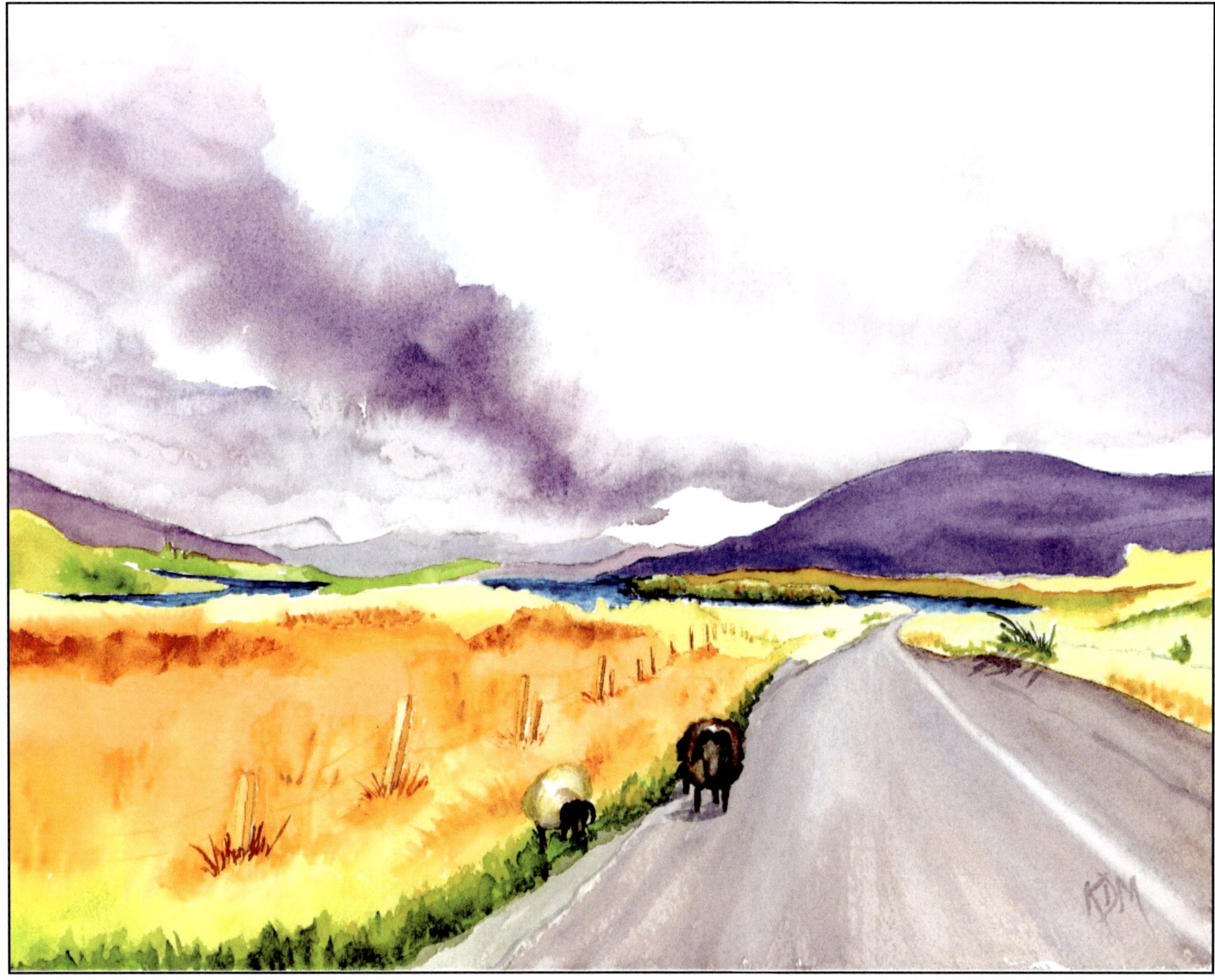

Artist's Reflection: *Driving Connemara's road 344 on a sunny late October day was such a breathtaking occasion. I can still feel the beauty of it now. Quiet, just us and the sheep, in the expansive valley. I pause to breathe this landscape into the deepest part of my body. The question of how a landscape forms a person's spiritual sensibilities is worth pondering. Surprisingly, I ponder endings here. The summer growing season is over. The grasses are dying. Yet the magnificent color reminds me that the Celts accepted death, not as frightening or ugly, but as an essential part of the grand whole of life. What a difference that belief could make today.*

Anointing

In this landscape of bog and rock,
   mountain and loch, and ancient trees pressed into peat,
   memories of forests lie buried.
Hibernian forests
   weighed down by ice and time
   crushed by sliding glaciers
   compressed into sources of fire.

Thriving on the shore of the loch
   stands this deep green survivor,
   strong, sheltering, tough,
   upright against Atlantic gales,
   ice-winds pounding like hammers,
   somehow avoiding the woodsman's axe.

Its limbs reach out for a blessing
   for continued strength
   to do what it is called to do
   shade and shelter
   exhale oxygen.

The tree asks for the blessing of light
   which pours through a cloud opening
   down a mountain pass
   to anoint this stalwart green reminder
   of the deep past of Connemara.

Poet's Notes: *As I regarded the dark green tree standing alone at the east end of Kylemore Lough, I felt its strength and determination just as I've thought the Irish in Western Ireland must have had to survive there. We were lucky to find a great little hotel on the lough and a room with this view. There was a large window ledge where Kathy could paint. I went down to a cozy gathering room with a peat fire and tea service (lovely) and sat and wrote and meditated and wrote . . .*

Shelter and Pause

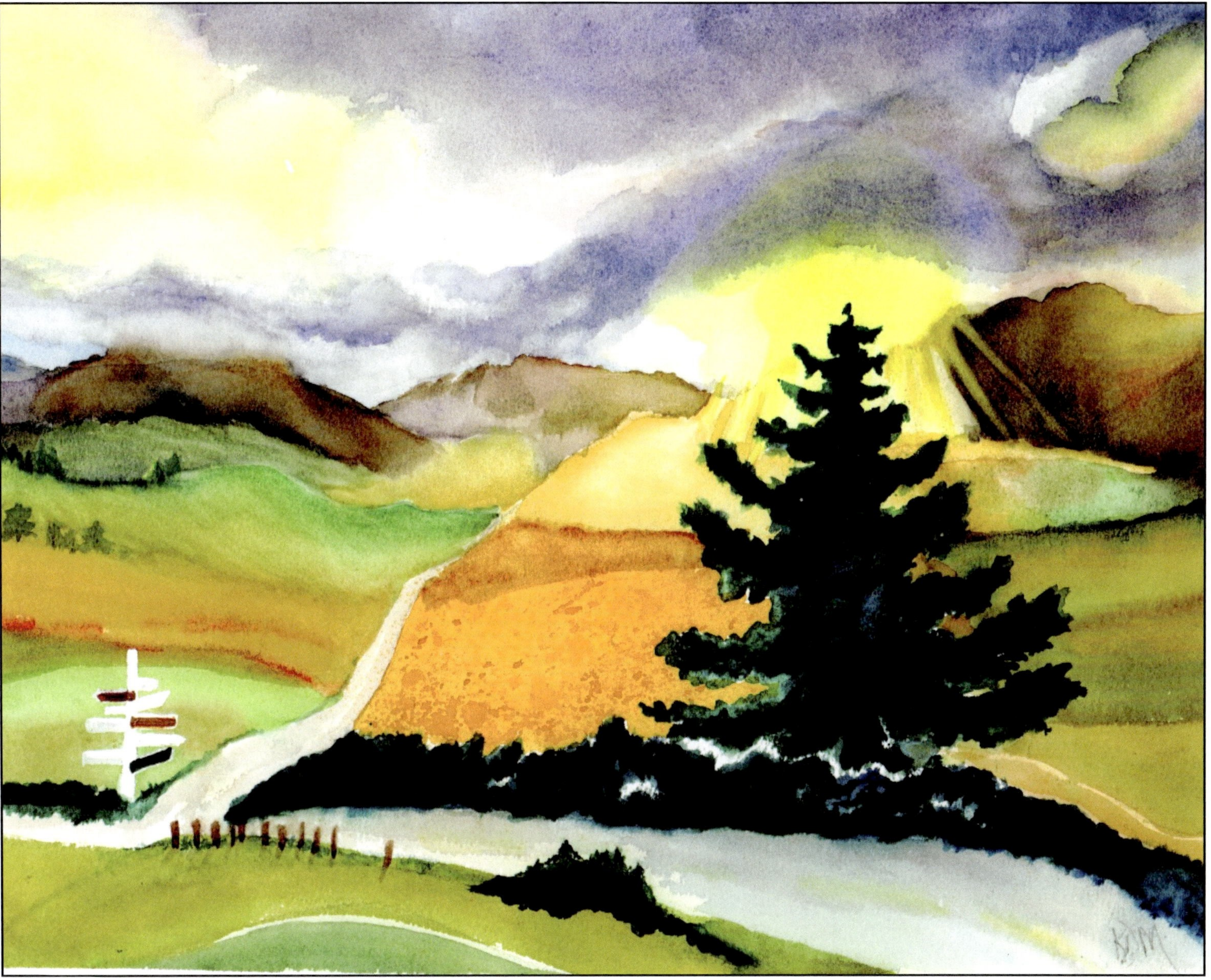

Artist's Reflection: *There it stood- a large lone pine in a deforested land, bushy with health. Growth is stubbornly saying yes to life. As the sky darkened, that bright beam of last sunlight caused me to pause- and in that moment of wonder, before I clicked the photo, there was the gift. I inhaled the rugged beauty of Connemara's survival.*

A Feather in Silence

The breath of the One, the Beloved,
    lowers, slowly, gently,
    a feather, to a resting place.

The feather then lies silent on a stone in the middle of
    a rivulet that crosses the path
    to Mamean Pass.

There is no human sound in this silence
    but there is a presence in Connemara's
    landscape,
    a quiet ensouled space – a rich silence
    and yet,

the breath of the One, the Beloved can shiver
    leaves and grasses, making green music
    to accompany the landscape

The breath of the One, the Beloved, at times
    makes mountains howl and moan,
    creates nature's orchestra in Connemara
    but can gently place a feather in a stream.

Beloved mystic, Meister Eckert, wrote
"Nothing resembles God so much as silence."
Here, in the silence and the music of
    Connemara,
Celts found the One, the Beloved, and home.

Poet's Notes*: The hike up to Mamean Pass is challenging – windy, rocky, sometimes wet. I was disappointed that we didn't see birds in this migratory passageway. There were not many living creatures to be seen other than a few other "hill walkers" and the charming 84-year-old Father Paddy who sprinted up the trail and left us in the dust (not really, it was rocky and wet!) when we stopped at a rock outcropping for a bit of shelter from the fierce wind. Water was seeping through the stones of the path, and that's where the feather lay, brought there by the wind. A feather in that silence, that windy silence, seemed an oddity in the spare elemental scene – rocks, dirt, water.*

Out of the Blue

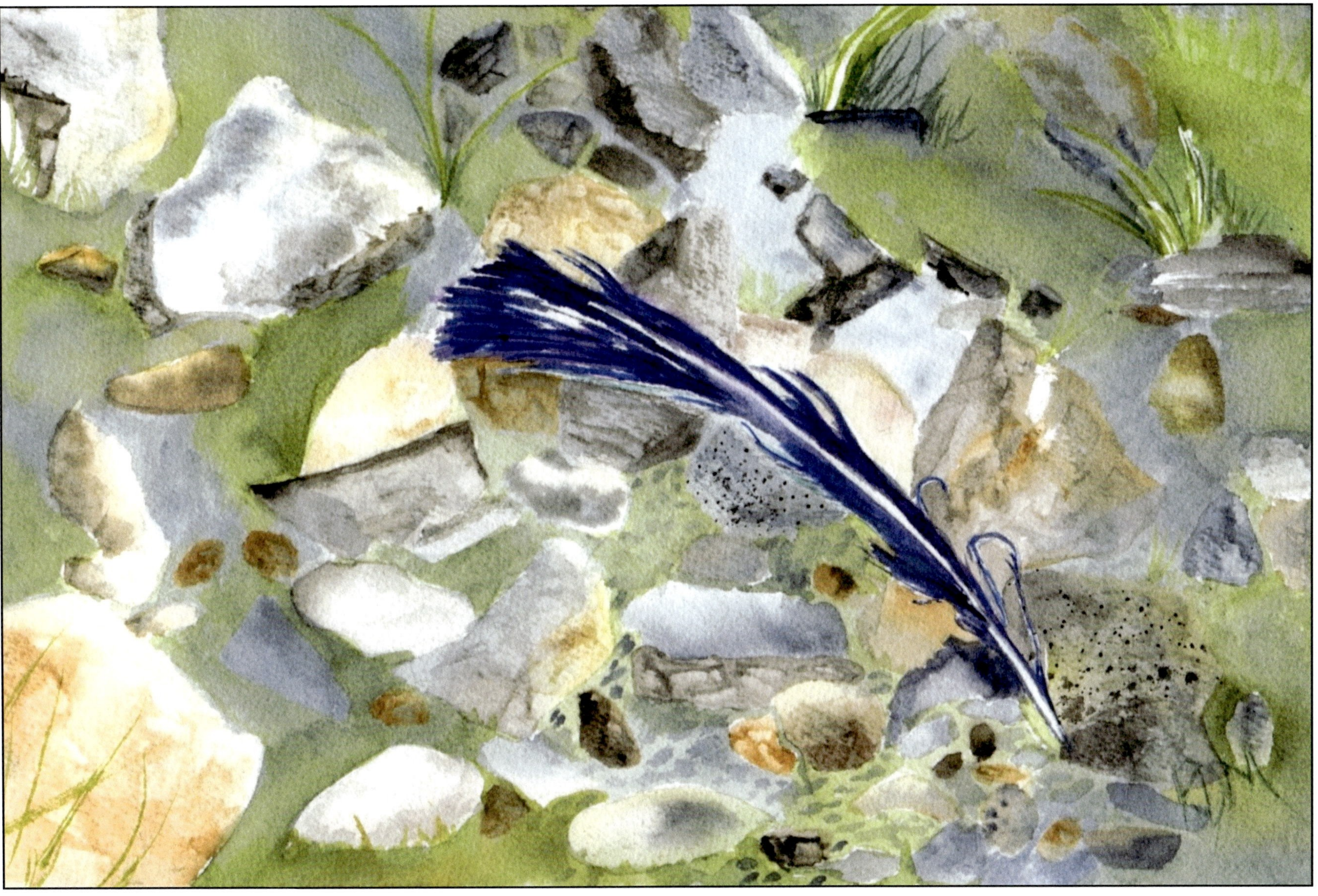

Artist's Reflection: *Impossibly rocky, that's what the pilgrimage trail of Mamean Passage is. Yet, there in the damp stream bed of pebbles and rocks lies a ragged blue-black crow feather. Remember, soaring is possible.*

Mamean Pass

Back pressed against stone chapel wall

eyes sweeping Connemara mountains

watery lowlands

sky with clouds and sun,

water pouring down mountains and

sitting on bogs,

sharp rock,

height, depth

mountains round me

extending from Mamean's chapel

left, right

as arms that shelter me,

from fierce morning winds

whipping through the pass,

arms that offer me an eternal embrace

of beauty, acceptance.

I begin to feel the embrace of this place,

its spirit,

and the secret wisdom, the holy silence

of wild and rugged Connemara.

The Beloved is here.

Poet's Notes: *After our climb to Mamean Pass, after Father Paddy and his companion had left for the pub at the other end of the trail, Kathy nestled on St. Patrick's Bed (a rock ledge) to draw. I found shelter on the south side of the little stone chapel, out of the wind. I sat on a concrete block, leaned against the chapel, and waited. It was a meditative, prayerful time as I alternately looked at the watery lowlands below, some of the Twelve Bens, pale blue sky with few clouds and in the distance, the deeper blue of the Atlantic – or closed my eyes. I waited. Then came with the word, embrace, a reference to the mountain arms that reach out to the left and right from the chapel where I sit. It seems a holy embrace within Creation.*

Mamean Vision Quest

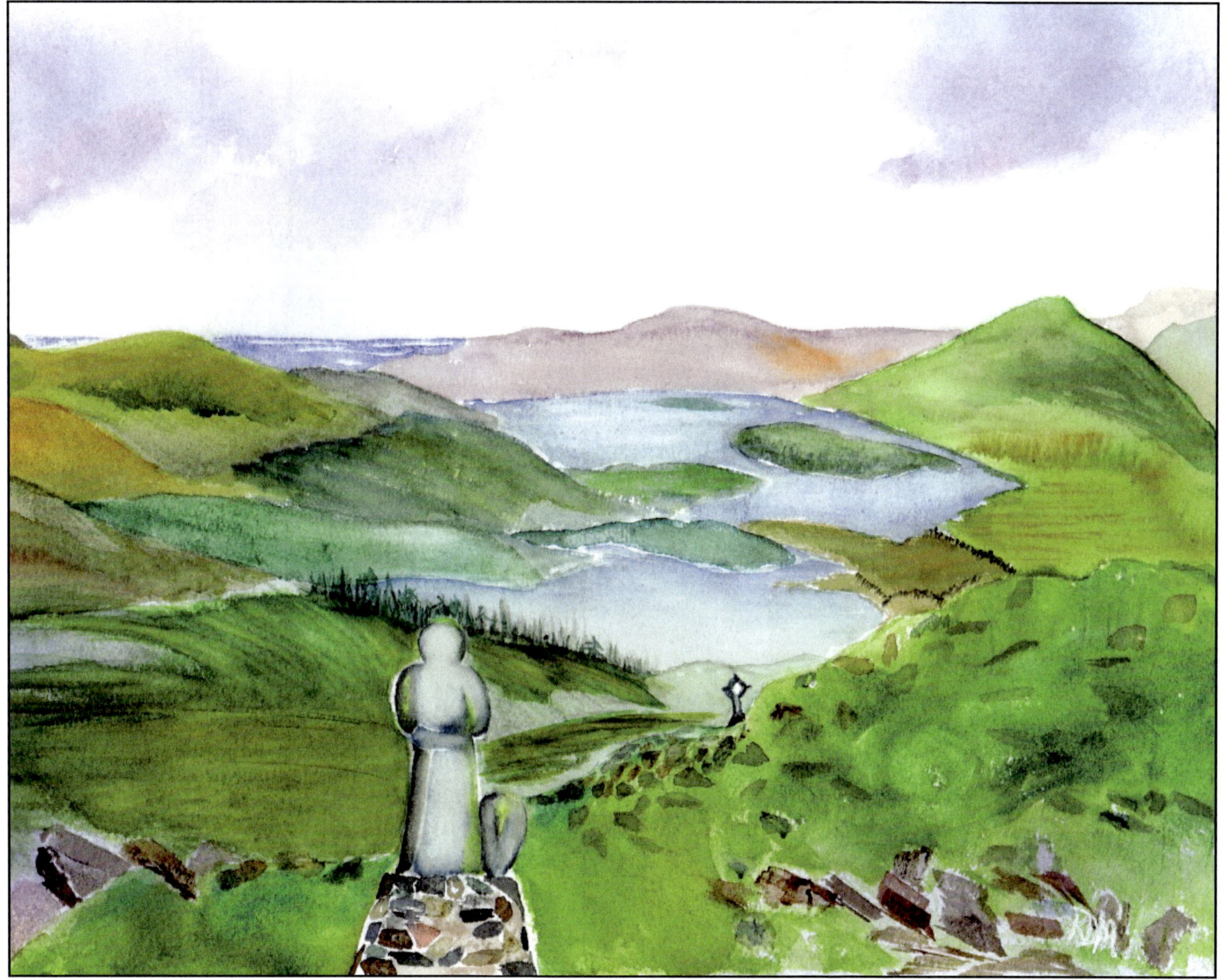

Artist's Reflection: *I knew from the moment of discovery that this hike had to be part of our pilgrimage. Just start, rest when needed, take the next step. So, companioned by ancient rocks, an elderly priest and a gusty wind, we climbed- adding our souls to the millennia of pilgrims. From the high chapel, I look out over lochs, mountains, valleys and ultimately the Wild Atlantic. I'd like to take this big a view of my inner landscape. It's easier to spend time in green moist places; harder in those sharp, shadow spots. What about the interior scrabble where loose rock causes missteps? I make an intention to consciously explore my distinctive inner landscape. Now, silence and the wild wind blowing where it will.*

Black Butter for Fire

The beauty of the black butter

  of the inner earth

  lies exposed

  as blocks of peat

  are dug for warmth which

    the chill Irish earth holds for its people.

The rich green turf stunningly crowns the black trenches

  of peat so thick, so thick,

  socompressedthat no oxygen remains.

But remains are found -

  bog bodies with skin and organs

  preserved in near perfection

    as this boggy peat preserves a source of warmth

    in its cold depths.

Poet's Notes: *Peat pits along the Connemara road are a stunning contrast – rich green grass crowning shiny black peat. I think of the hard work to cut blocks of peat and that this black earth became fuel. The peat fires in the two Connemara hotels where we stay produce steady heat and little smoke. The history of peat is fascinating – its transformation from living material to this rich source of heat much needed in this cool damp climate.*

Turf Cutting

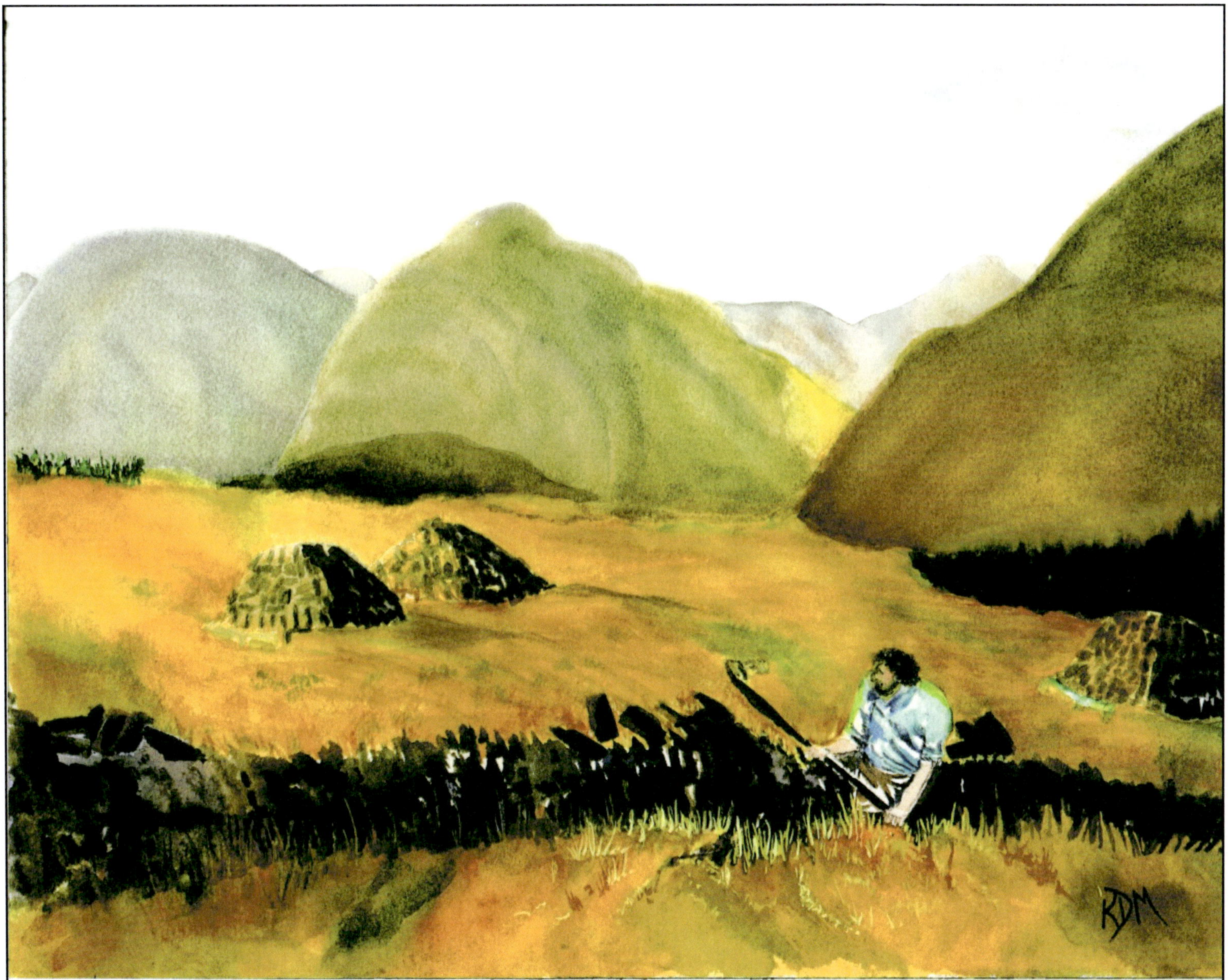

Artist's Reflection: *The rhythm of hard chopping in the dark turf becomes a meditation -deep truths –history –creation. Making fire from pressed, rotted vegetation- now there's a story! Long burning peat with more dependability gives generous heat. Sitting by the peat fires, we talk with strangers as we travel around -- day and night pass, it's surprising and good.*

Sunrise at Renvyle House

The Great and First Imagination

    paints the dawn at Renvyle

    as the world awakens.

The moon holds yet a tea cup of darkness,

    moon's companion, just before it begins

       to fade.

Diffuse brilliant light splashes a deep palette

    on everything it touches,

      clouds and cottages,

    mountain, rocks, water,

    soft butter white

    darkening to gentle ochre gold,

    purple, violet, last midnight's

      blue, indigo.

Nothing stays the same

    at this tender threshold of transfiguration

    between night and day.

Colors fade or deepen,

every object shining back the color it rejects

    in fresh transformation of ancient into new.

Poet's Notes: *Kathy and I planned to gather our thoughts for a day and two nights at Renvyle House, famous as the hotel where W. B. Yeats spent his honeymoon. Kathy had been to Renvyle House the year before and knew it had space, solarium-like, where we could begin to process our experiences at the end of our trip. We were up at dawn to pull open the curtains of the almost room-wide windows facing east. We were transfixed at the color show the emerging sun made on every visible thing from the mountains north, to Killary Fjord to the little cottages nearby. There was a continual color transformation – our theme word for the trip and our work.*

Ahh! Awe!

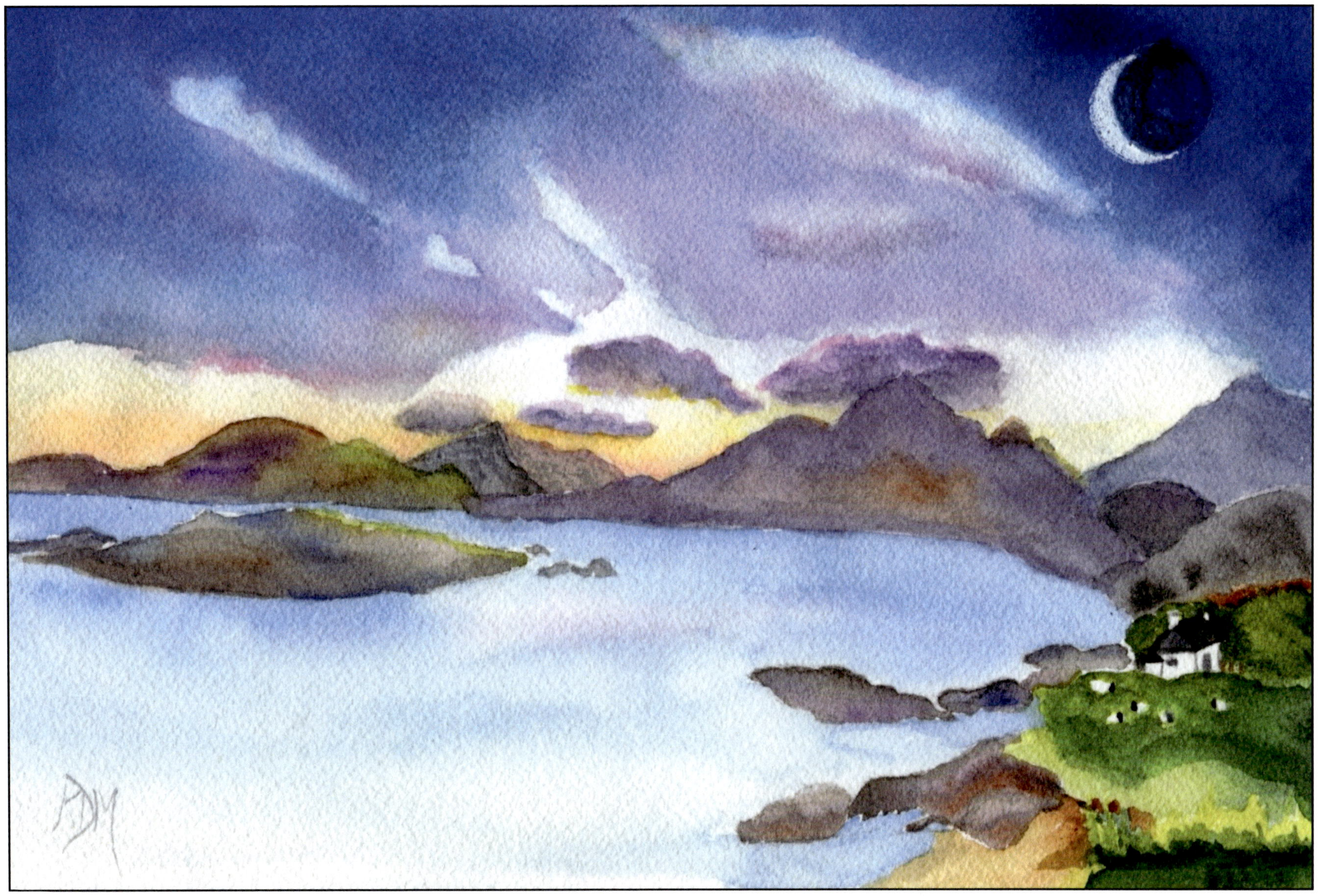

Artist's Reflection: *I love sunrise. Most days, I pause and notice it gratefully. I'll never forget waking up in room 54 of Renvyle House to see a perfectly clear sunrise about to happen. With warm bedspreads draped over our shoulders and a cup of hot tea in our hands, we witnessed the sunrise as the crescent moon hovered at the big sky's edge. The mountains glowed. The icy waters glimmered.*

Spirit in the Hearth

As the Celtic mother smoored her fire,

    blessing it to smolder through the night,

    her hearth and home demonstrated

    the warmth of the love

    that has lived there.

In the hearth peat bricks provide

      the constant warmth of a steady fire

Perhaps burning peat

    cut from cold ground

    made of eons of plants and pressure,

    change from their cold waiting

    to unfaltering heat in order to

    warm the bodies of those whose love

    infuses the spirit of the home.

Poet's Notes: *I was surprised at peat fire. It didn't roar as do wood fires at our cabin nor did it stutter hot then weak warm. It was simply constant. When I wrote this poem, I was thinking of the contrast of the cold ground and warmth of spirit in the home. Smooring the fire was an old Scots custom to tamp down the fire for the night and was done with words invoking the Trinity.*

Peat Fires

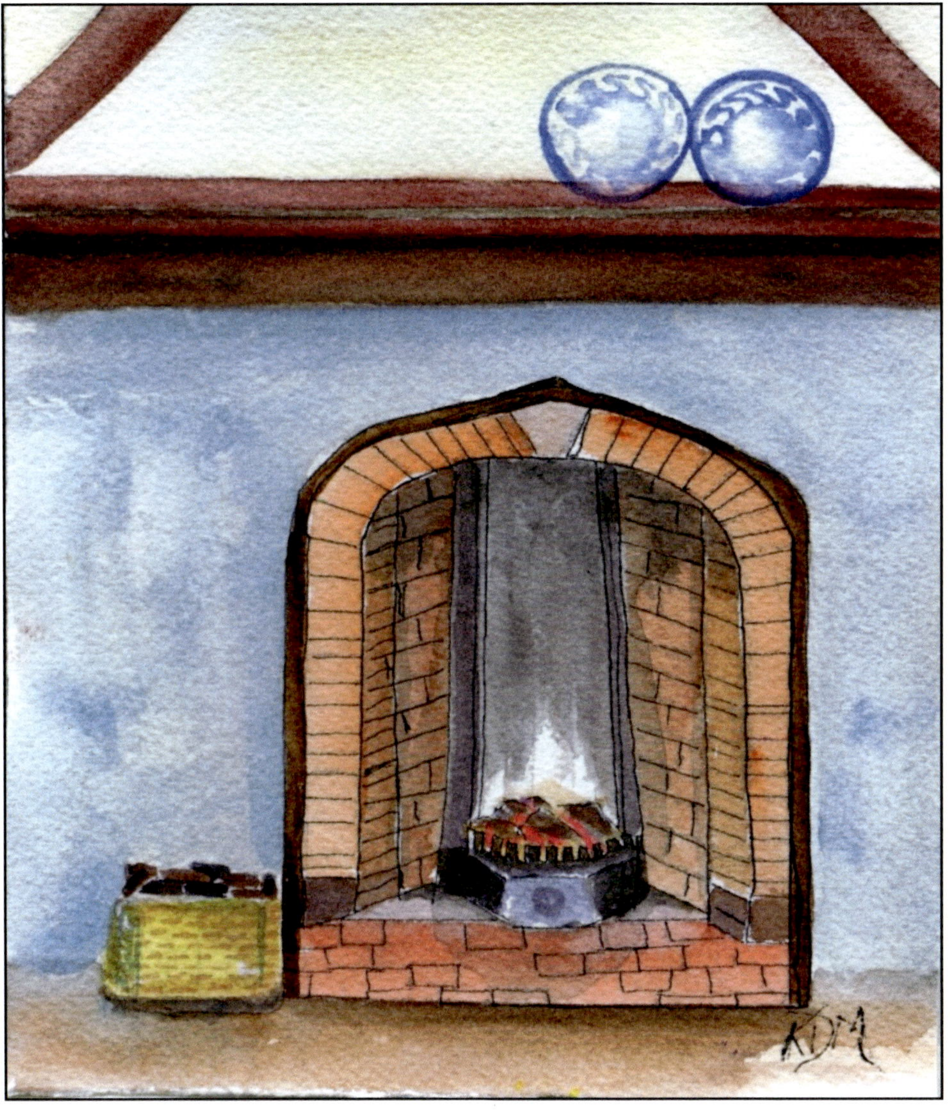

Artist's Reflection: *Fireplaces seem like places of exchange to me. Sitting by the peat fire, I breathe in the distinctive smoke smell that softly fills the comfortable room here at Renvyle House. It's the ancient vegetation, pressed to peat, now burned to give warmth-Exchange. It's the lonely widow who, unexpectedly, sits beside me to chat-Exchange. It's the air, cool on this late fall night, meeting the hot smoke rising in the chimney-Exchange. It's energy of all sorts meeting, mingling, moving. There's soul here and I love it! Now that our Pilgrimage is nearly over, I am living more deeply. Deeply Living. Deeply giving it away. The Great Exchange.*

Luisne and the Spirit of Being There

The early light shifts, changing hues

   as if a painter is still playing with the palette,

   revealing the natural world through a series of tints and tones

   'til the light decides at last to shine full force.

The sheep have progressed from dull

   gray to brilliant white,

   stones now shadowy grays from dusty charcoal

   and grasses, trees, bushes so dull

   shine back now their vibrant greens

   in response to the light from the dome of the sky.

It is almost the fifth day

   when the light, the waters, the land

   and the living creatures form a tableau of wonder

   that waits for Adam's eye.

Poet's Notes: *Another beautiful sunrise, a primal experience really. I was thinking of wonder, experiencing it as a well-traveled person, and "wondered" what it was like for the first sentient beings to see such beauty and transformation. I had heard the word "luisne" as meaning color or glow. That certainly fit this sunrise.*

Luisne

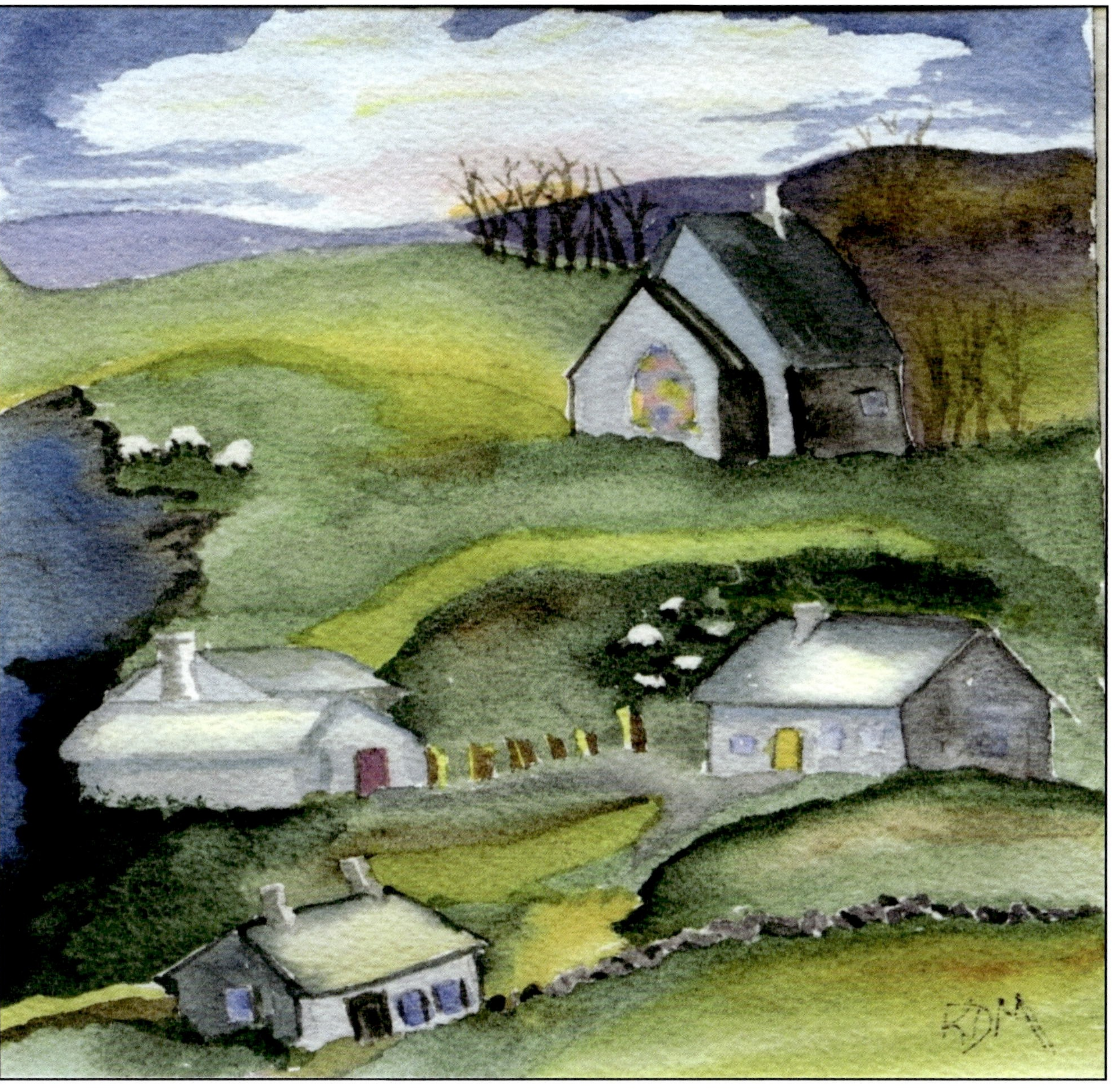

Artist's Reflection: *There overlooking the cobalt waters of Killary Fjord and the hefty mountains, still dark, the day's first glow of light's return awakened me. A new chance-- New possibilities? For those living in pain, what does "luisne" mean? A cry for relief? A determination, calling a difference in? Here lives hope- for us all.*

Bleak Connemara

Something is missing in this landscape.

Yes, there are sheep, in their trance-like grazing

   but the abandoned house, slowly crumbling

   the boggy grasslands uninviting

   the absence of human creation or activity

   such bleakness

     yet

We could summon artists, poets, mystics to

   remedy that perspective.

They might tell us that

   the grasses whisper, the water gurgles music,

   and the mountains echo,

   "We nourished, we fed all the eyes, and we filled all hearts.

   This is creation, the big Celtic book,

   fecund and full of spirit."

Poet's Notes: *Driving south of Maam Cross (a crossroads community of one big hotel and a few outbuildings), we were looking for the lowlands seen from Mamean Pass.   We entered a watery, grassy, unpopulated world. Yet looking west, north and east we saw the mountains – the Twelve Bens, Croagh Patrick over this foreground of bleakness. I wanted to express the mystery of divine revelation written about by Celtic Christian scholars, revelation occurring even here. Ancient Celtic Christian teachers wrote about learning from and honoring the little book (the Bible) and the big book (creation).*

Those Sheep Belong

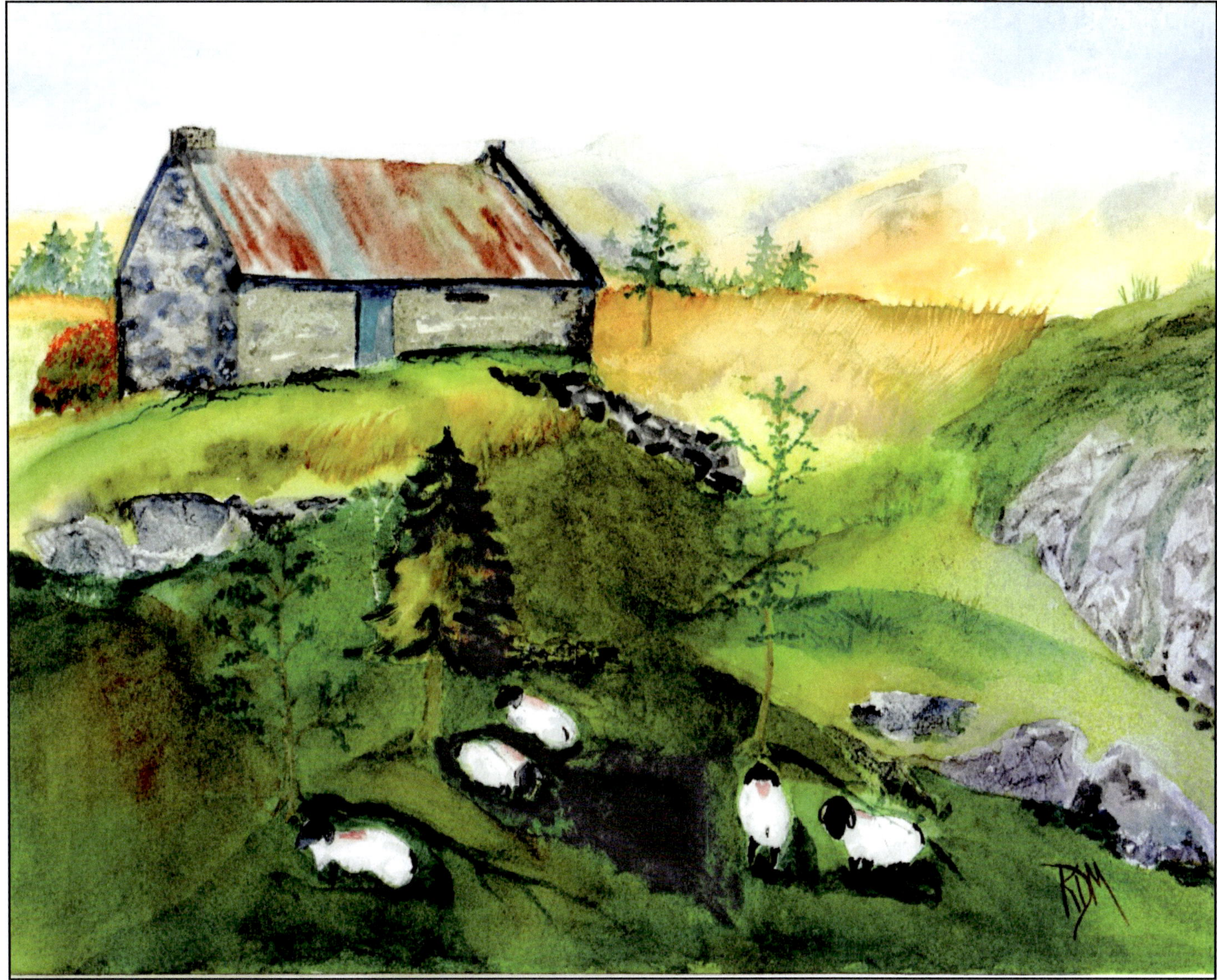

Artist's Reflection: *Driving down that unnamed road, how quickly it becomes isolated and quite desolate. And then, there they are, those sheep. They are branded with paint to say, "I belong" even in the lonely rugged landscape. No matter how difficult the landscape of life is, each of us is branded by God. No matter how lonely the path, grace is there to support my being true. The call is to authenticity- the quest to be who I was designed to be... Branded by God.*

Stillness and Rythym

"If we look with God's eye, nothing on Earth is ugly." –Pelagius

Sense the silence

  in this utterly still landscape

  marked sheep chewing

    meditatively

  the breeze stilled too

  diffuse light painting rocks and mountains.

Yet there is a rhythm in this quiet panorama

  a sense of movement

  not simply drifting diffuse color-loaded clouds

  but rocks and mountains

  leaning toward each other

  encircling the saddened house

  the munching sheep, the grasses, tree, bog.

This landscape could companion the hermit.

  As he looked out from his little beehive hut

  he could sense a spirit-infused earth and sky.

Perhaps nature was his anam cara.

Poet's Notes: *The bleakness of Connemara south of Maam Cross was disheartening, yet I wanted to think of how it must have been different for those hermits and seekers who understood the Celtic concept of God-filled creation.*

Sturdy Comfort

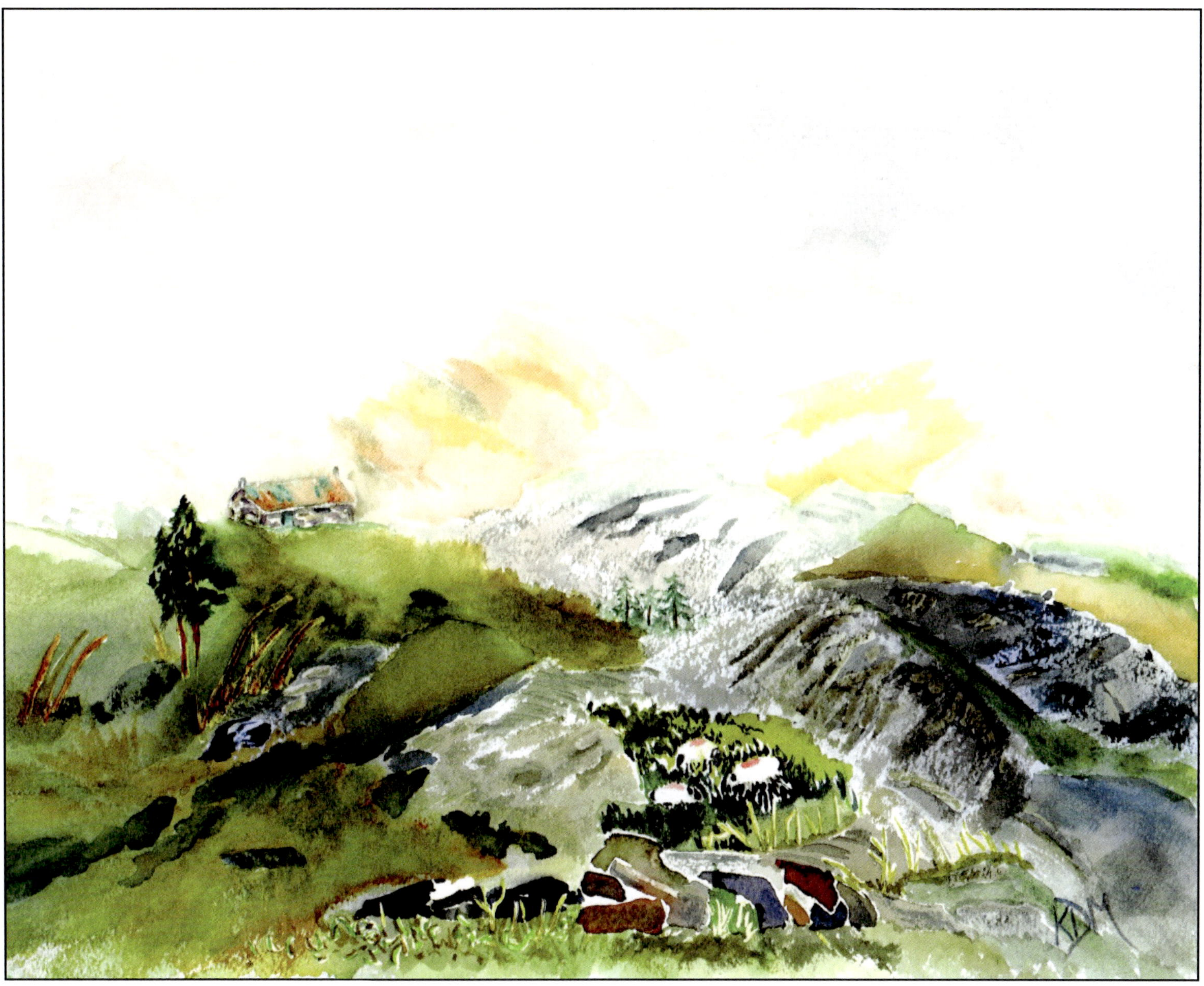

Artist's Reflection: *Home is in a rock cottage with people making memories, passing memories on. Who will listen? Who will clear the fog? Only the heart can hear, and with the imagination can carve out the story.*

Newgrange

Deep Wisdom

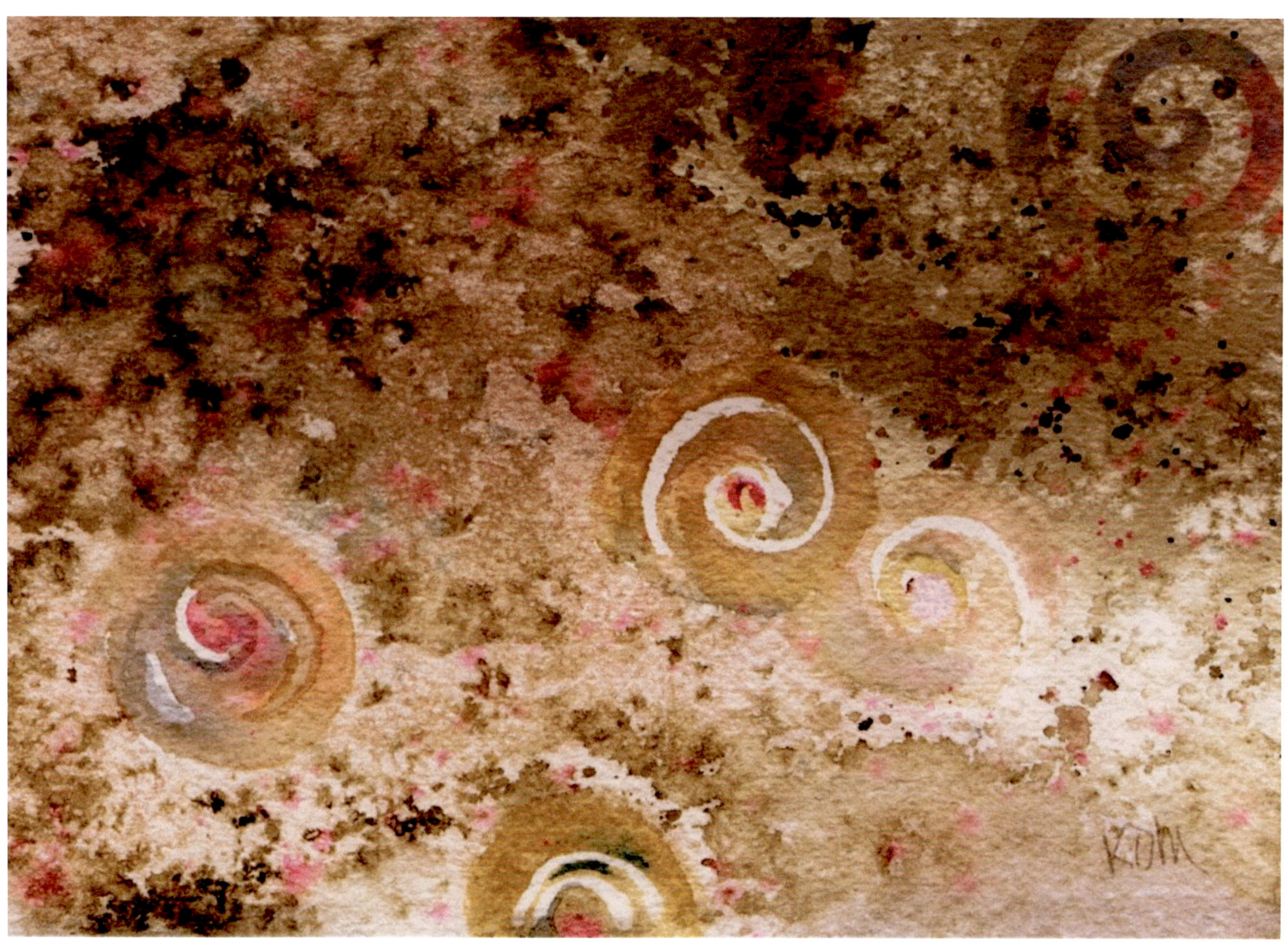

When was the Iron Age, exactly? What was life like in the Neolithic Era of 3,500- 2,700 BCE? It's hard to imagine.

On our last day we visit the UNESCO World Heritage Sites of Newgrange and Knowth in the lovely Boyne Valley north of Dublin. These huge grassy mounds are only part of the ancient and rich history of this fertile green landscape in County Meath.

Called passage tombs, Newgrange, Knowth, and Dowth were rediscovered in the 1960s. Knowth is smaller and probably dates from 2,500-2,000 BCE. Dowth is not yet open to the public. The research and recovery continues.

There, not far from the banks of the southwest flowing Boyne River, is the giant inscribed stone boulder that guards the entrance of Newgrange. There, we follow the long narrow passage inward to the underground room with its three adjoining rooms. There, are the mysterious carvings that are older than the Egyptian Pyramids.

Our wonderful guide tells us that we should walk here with reverence because these are hallowed grounds where important ceremonies and events have taken place since prehistory.

We are silent as we consider the roof box above the entrance which lets the rising sun shine into the deep center room of Newgrange only on the Winter Solstice each year. We learn that Knowth is also built facing east-west.

We slowly walk around each mound looking with awe at the size of and inscriptions on the mammoth boulders. Somehow they were moved here to this important site since the type of rock is found many miles away.

Although no written records of this society exist, this seems to be a culture that found meaning in the practical observance of natural seasonal cycles. They were able to spend time and energy building enormous tombs which may show the spiritual importance of life and death. Light and dark, spiral circles, creativity in design and decoration are all themes that will carry forward to the Celtic sensibilities which will follow thousands of years later.

Neart

Spirit dances
through fern and flower,
feathered song and rock,
day's bright eye,
night's winking lights.

Spirit hums through
mounds, tunnels,
fish, bouncing lambs,
sturdy limbs, steady trunks,
in the air, clouds, and rain,
in the seas and torrential rivers.

Spirit of change and growth,
energy of creation,
you know this Celtic soil eternally

and this people who have you
in their bones and have honored
and, yes, loved you through
all of spiraling time.

Spirit – love energy –
above us, below us,
in front of and behind us,
on the left and the right of us,
enfolding and eternally within,
all things.

Poet's Notes: *I read that "neart" is Gaelic for God's creative energy which I think of as flowing through everything. Celts felt the Holy to be immanent, not remote and hostile (thanks to St. Patrick). I wrote to celebrate all creation as Spirit-filled.*

Time Will Tell

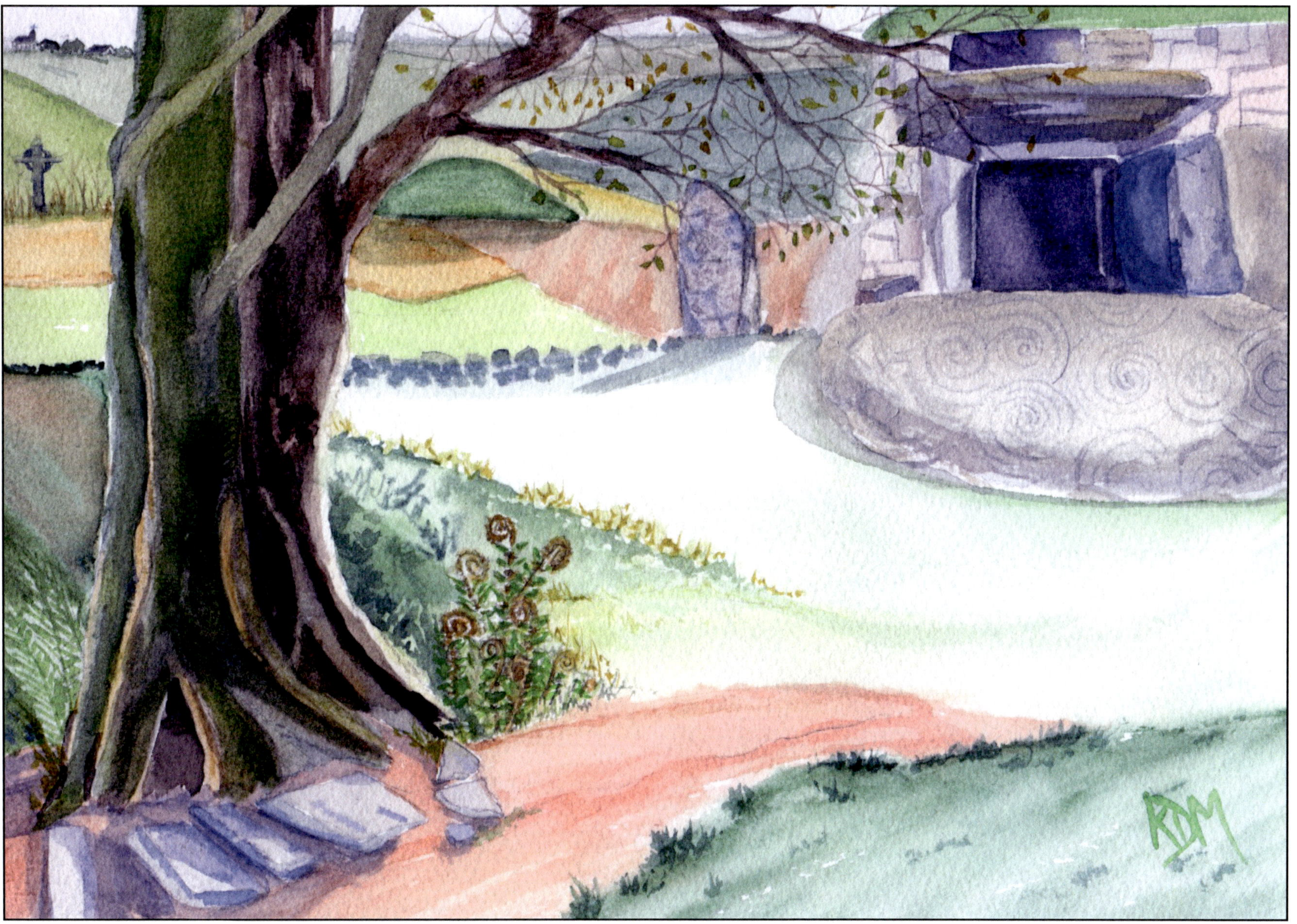

Artist's Reflection: *Arriving at Newgrange and Knowth, the high green rounded mounds remind me of a pregnant woman's belly, grace-filled curves. I know they're called "passage tombs," but what if the sublime intuition that motivated these epic building efforts was not only death but birth? Facing east and the rising sun, they point to a new day, a new life.*

The Center of Things

Follow the alternating contrast
  light dark light dark
  that draws you in
  to the center of things
  where the meaning is.
In that center a cantilevered
  ceiling holds inscribed messages,
   hidden.
Look for them.
Follow the pattern first, learning
  as you go,

understanding more
and deeper
through this squared spiral
Celtic to the core
yet aligned with other
ancients seeking order.
Go deeper for meaning.
Think of Velásquez' 'Las meninas'
A painting with depth and contrast
    and
  innocence and life,
  messages
  at the center of things.

Poet's Notes: *There was something so arresting about looking down the passageway into this Neolithic mound at New Grange and being impelled to the center. I was reminded of a Mayan pyramid passageway deep and deeper to the center where the red jaguar was. I was struck by the improbable likeness to Velasquez' painting "Las meninas" with its light dark contrast giving the painting depth and showing the painter himself prominent but obscure on the left.*

Narrow Path

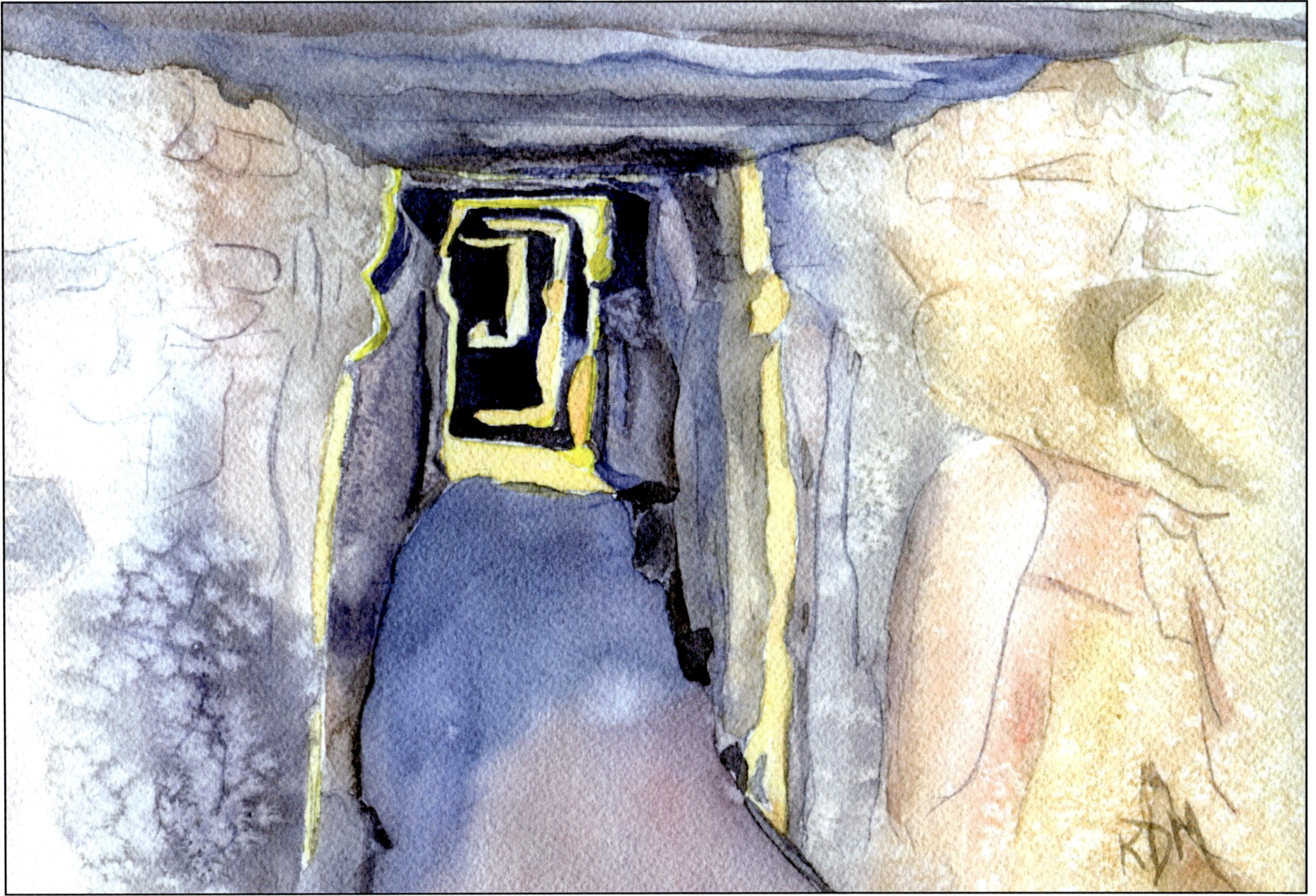

Artist's Reflection: *Inching our way through the narrow, slightly uphill, weaving path toward the central rooms of Newgrange, I'm grateful for the occasional lights that guide us inward. It is deep and dark and very quiet in here. The boulders that form the walls are rough and poke at my shoulders and arms as I pass. Seeds and babies grow in the dark. Then there is the hard work of finding their way toward the light through the scratchy soil or narrow birth canal. They adapt, turn, move along, slower or more quickly, until finally, this indirect route leads them to break free into the light having already learned some things about survival.*

Remember

Layer within layer within layer
of rich intense life
passes through us
we, the unaware,
with our deep joys, deep sorrows

It comes to this,
Remember.
Remember our beloveds, sources
of joy and sorrow and love.

Shall we wait for Samhain
for the veil to thin
to be with them again?
No.

Remember.

Poet's Notes: *My continuing study of Celtic spirituality and myths has enriched my own spiritual life and connected me to ancestors from whom I was cut off by migration and lack of family story. How the celebration of Samhain resonates with All Saints Day and Days of the Dead! How strong is the Mexican practice of remembrance! In our rush to ignore death, I fear we lack a practice of deep remembrance.*

Remembering

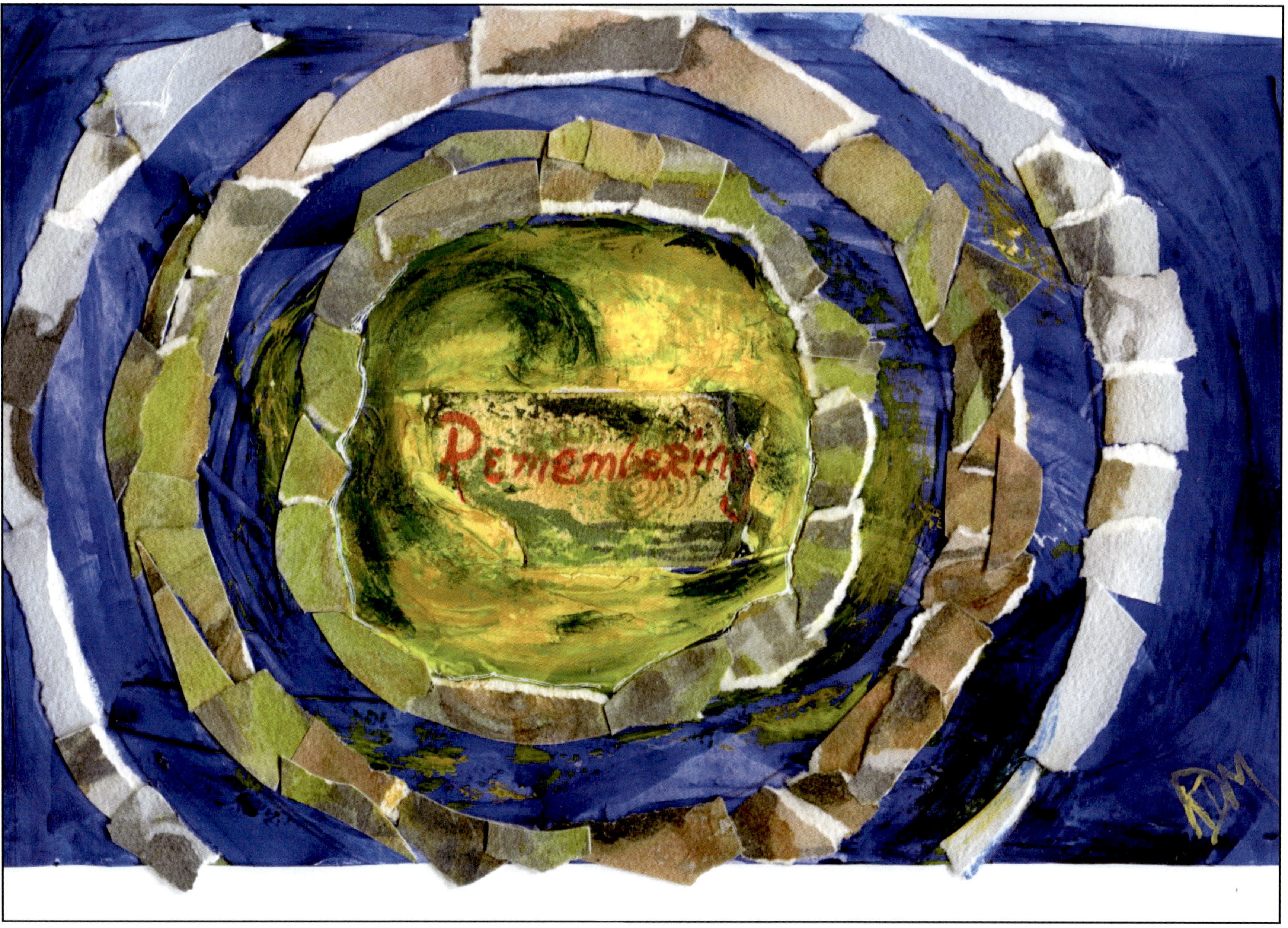

Artist's Reflection: *Things are not always as they seem. Today's assumptions are not Truth. May we have the humility to be curious. May we be willing to take the time to ponder the beauty we observe. May we honor what fits of the ancient wisdom embedded in the natural world and our DNA.*

Tender Fire

Red, fire of creation,

  accepts all colors

    but red,

      sends back red light,

        a message of heat, growth, danger.

Yet here in rich wild western Ireland

  jeweled

    flowers

      hang:

  red and purple fuschia,

    a tender fire,

  hot only with expansive growth,

  surviving wild winds and rains.

Thriving, it dances with high hats

    and swirling red skirts like

        colorful Sufis of the Burren.

Poet's Notes: *I have marveled so at lush fuchsia on the western coast of Ireland and on the Scottish Isle of Iona. They flourish and grow as tall as camellias in our southern state. Yet we can only grow them as hanging potted plants. And, when I saw Kathy's painting, which I love, I suddenly saw the likeness to the Sufi whirling dervish – in shape if not in color. I wrote to honor both the painting and the plant.*

Fuchsia

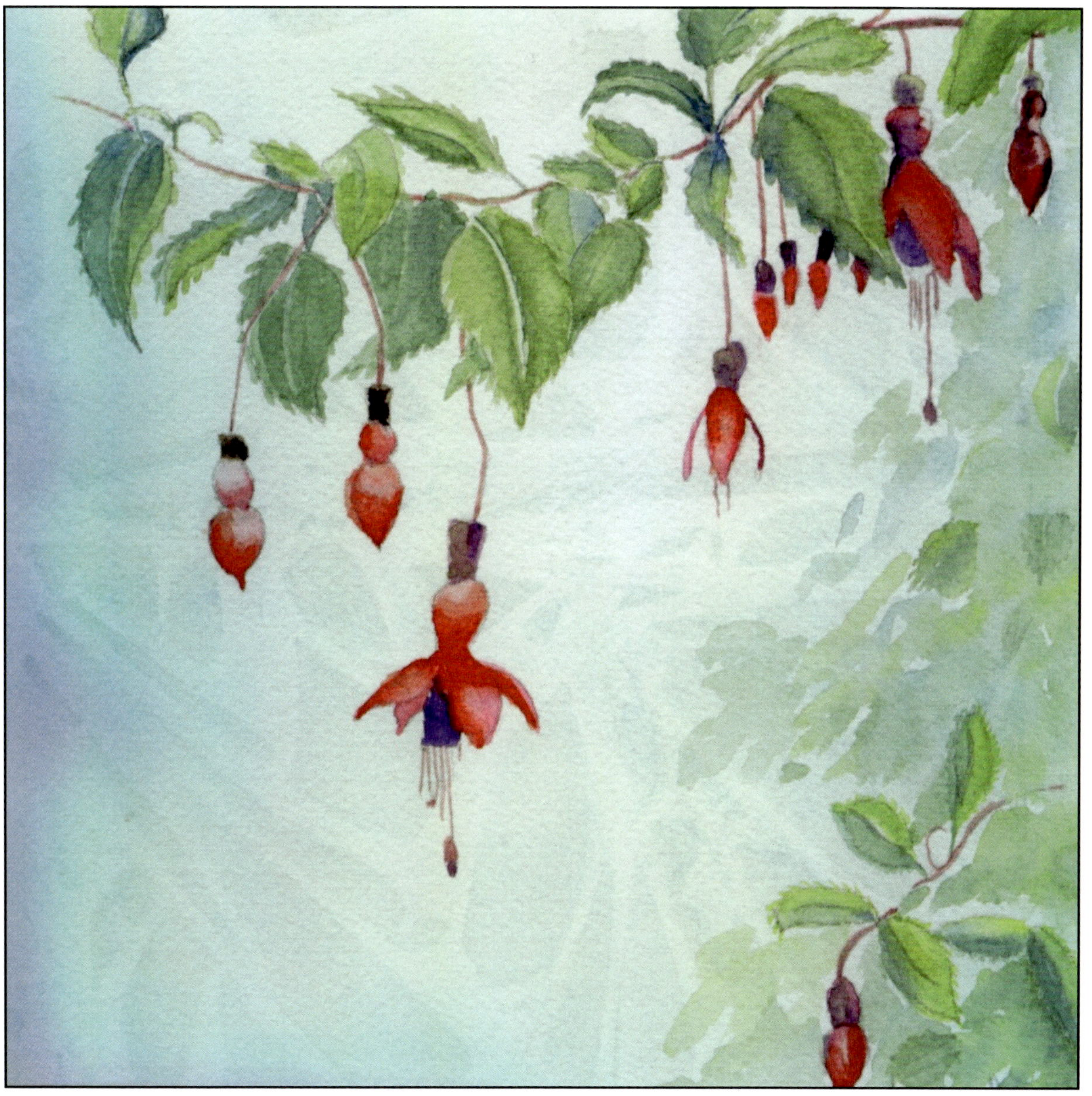

Artist's Reflection: *They make me smile, those dancing fuchsia blossoms with intricate petals. I remember a conversation with a stranger at Brandon Bay. It was twenty years ago. He pressed me to return to Ireland promising great hedges of fuchsia flowers, when the time is right. It sounded outlandish-magical. And so, I remembered and dreamed of fuchsia hedges. Now, not only once have I walked among the blooming fuchsia hedges, but twice. What is scarce can become abundant. Hang on to your dreams.*

Afterwords

(Kathy) Landscape Musings

There is an old joke about a Thermos bottle that keeps hot food hot and cold food cold. The naive questioner wonders, "How does it know?" That joke, a favorite of my father's, comes to mind as I hold and now, begin to attend to my impressions gathered on our pilgrimage to Ireland. My question has been, "How did the landscape contribute to the evolution of Celtic Spirituality, its worldview, its theology?" Landscapes are all around all of us all the time. Some people are profoundly influenced by weather, trees, animals, sunsets; some people hardly notice them. How do we know? What causes a person to pay attention to the surrounding world?

Celtic prayers are full of meeting God in the elements of earth. Passed down from mother to child over generations, the honor given to this life was framed by finding the Holy in the natural during ordinary life in their homes, yards and chores. A welcoming posture becomes a threshold through which anyone can pass and hopefully meet the Numinous, even experiencing "thin places" where the natural and spiritual worlds merge. Curiosity leads to engagement and a more expansive life experience. Even more important though, is reverence, that is deep regard or respect.

- Imagine being a natural storyteller born into a devout family which sees miracles in the stars at night or the presence of the saints in the hospitality of neighbors. Mysteries can be explored in tales told around the fire at night.

- Imagine walking past acres of rocks to retrieve the family cows from their summer pastures. Seasonal changes brought preparations that became rituals and times to contemplate thresholds -- a favorite Celtic theme.

- Imagine the hard work of digging potatoes or cutting turf, digging deep into the shell of the earth that supports life. Here is the opportunity to observe the many things one did know and wonder about the many things one did not know; pondering inner and outer landscapes.

Following the thread of one's longing can create a pathway to a meaningful life. An energized sense of vitality is a touchstone marking that pathway. It is also, for me, a definition of beauty; no counterfeits here. The sense of vitality I feel every time I travel, every time I learn while traveling, is one of the ways I "know."

As a woman, my style is to take in the new place, hold it (like a gestation), and then notice what emerges for me. It's rather like planting a seed then waiting for it to sprout from the mysterious alchemy of soil and sun. Waiting and silence are requirements for this ongoing experiment. By asking the landscape question in the context of Celtic Spirituality, I was actually asking the question of myself. I do not live in the physical landscape that formed me as a child. I did not choose where I live now. Yet, I have thrived here where the regional story is not my story. "How do I know?" How does that special knowing evolve? Somehow in meditating on this mysterious equation, a clarity arises. The landscape is a living organism and humans are formed from it. In some mysterious way every part of the universe is already at home in us. The wisdom of appreciating this mystery is a matter of the heart, then the mind, I think. Fortunately, there are wise ones and storytellers who help the rest of us appreciate what we, otherwise, would have missed.

Being in Ireland has helped me make meaning where there were questions before. I have loved the hours of silence spent painting the landscapes happily experienced in the Burren, Lough Corrib, Connemara, and Newgrange. Here is a fertile ground of spirituality for me, generating an enlarged sense of energized vitality, a celebration of beauty. My love of nature was given livelier meaning when I gladly stepped through the threshold after discovering Celtic Spirituality. Now I can better recognize and choose Spirit's prompts with respect, creativity and generosity.

With a reverent bow to Ireland and her magic, and to those wise Celtic souls, ancient and modern, I am grateful.

(Patty)

"In you all things consist and hang together: The very atom is light energy, the grass is vibrant, the rocks pulsate. All is in flux; turn but a stone and an angel moves…."(George MacDonald)

The West of Ireland is magical. It is soulful. And there were certainly stones in the Burren and angels on our shoulders as we investigated a part of the Burren that we'd read about. We did not have an agenda in our pilgrimage, other than the places we wanted to experience: the Caher Valley, Loch Corrib, Connemara, and finally Newgrange.

The Celts made pilgrimages all over the island and beyond. What were they searching for? If I were an early Celtic Christian, I would have been looking for a blessing from a holy well or site of a saint, but I would also look to be fed spiritually from the countryside. The land, the air, the sky is full of spirit. The Celts believed that the Holy was in everything which is panentheism not pantheism.

If the reader can pause to pay attention wherever in nature they are, there will be a reward–a depth of understanding, a breath of beauty. The Celtic blessings and prayers that I've found in books like *Celtic Christian Spirituality* or *Listening for the Heartbeat of God*, have opened my mind and heart to receive when I pay attention – when I am awake! Slowing down, simply being in the moment helped me experience this special land. The profound spirituality in the writings of early Celtic Christians–letters, prayers, hymns–show a way of living in Creation, not above it or controlling it. The Breastplate (or lorica) of St. Patrick calls the following for his shield: sun, moon, fire, lightning, wind, ocean, all from the physical world.

As much as I experienced viscerally our pilgrimage in this part of Ireland, my response was words. What else could I do to impart the gift of this trip to you, dear Reader? So, I remain hopeful that the words and paintings of this book will lead you to experience a Celtic sense of wonder in everything: the human, creation and the Divine.

Itinerary

Day 1- We drive from Dublin to Ballyvaughan, via the truck loading district somewhere outside of Dublin. Lunch at the Streetside Café in Enfield. After checking in at the Ballyvaughan Lodge, walk to dinner at Wild Way Pub.

Day 2- After a wonderful breakfast served by Gerry, our host, we walk the muddy Loop Trail. Meeting a forest ranger and talking with her about the area and her work is a pleasant surprise. Moving on, we listen to mooing cows, taste wild blackberries, notice snails and spiral lichen on the big rocks, seek the ocean view. We drive slowly down the oceanside road past Fanore admiring the karst landscape of the Burren. We finish the day with dinner at Monks on the Pier.

Day 3- Gerry and Pauline, our B&B hosts, talk about famous people "in this very house." We buy tin whistles at the little but lovely Ballyvaughan store. This is how we will find each other should we get separated. We purposely will not use our cell phones. Back to the Caher River, today we drive to the top ridge, remembering David Whyte's phrase about being "appreciators of horizons." (*River Flow*, p. 286) We walk the high pastures road. Returning to the curve in the river, Kathy paints the view to Galway Bay. Patty walks and explores. The day ends with a long dark drive to Ballycurrin House on Lough Corrib. Dinner is delicious at Angler's Rest in Headford.

Day 4- We walk to the lighthouse on Lough Corrib where Kathy sits in the chill and paints while Patty explores the shoreline and the Norman ruins. Then back to Ballycurrin House to write and paint over tea in the pleasant great room on a chilly overcast day. Remembering Mary Oliver's words, "Pay attention, be astonished, tell about it." (*Devotions*, pg. 105), we begin a list of themes that are emerging for us and end the day with a perfect sunset.

Day 5- Mamean Pilgrimage Route. It's a gorgeous day, bright and windy. After waiting for sheep to mosey off the road, we meet Father Paddy and Barbara who join us climbing to the top of Mamean Pilgrimage Pass. We made it! Blessings and singing around St Patrick's statue, Holy Well water collected, we bid farewell to our new friends. After lunch and quiet time, we meet and talk with a couple who are "hillwalkers." There's a party at Ballycurrin House tonight, with singing, talking and terrible jokes.

Day 6- We leave Ballycurrin House a day early (boiler problems). We eat lunch at Peacock's in Maam Cross while enjoying good local music. It's a gorgeous drive on Rt 344 to Kylemore Pass Hotel with a room overlooking the mountains and lake, a great painting opportunity. Patty has writing time and tea by the peat fire. We're the only guests. Dinner is a delicious smoked salmon salad. We have a great chat with Rose the cook who may be a relative of Kathy's.

Day 7- We start out for Killary Fjiord, Leenane, and Connemara National Park on a pretty pale day. Later, arriving at Renvyle House, it's a thrill to look out the window of room 54 and see a view so perfectly beautiful we think we are dreaming! The evening is pleasant with a play by Eammon Gammon and dinner in the Pub.

Day 8- It's a day of rest and re-collecting which starts with an amazingly clear and beautiful sunrise. The bright red geraniums in the sunny conservatory are so welcoming. Friends from Ballycurrin House show up by surprise. Yes, Renvyle House does have one of the best club sandwiches in the world. We walk the grounds and especially enjoy the rocky beach. Rory Makem, Tommy Makem's son, and the Spain Brothers are playing great music in the Pub. We have not put our thoughts and paintings together as we had planned, but we've had such a memorable pilgrimage. Tomorrow we leave for Newgrange in the beautiful Boyne Valley, then Dublin and home.

Day 9- It's a rainy day for our long drive back toward Dublin and Newgrange. On an impulse, we explore a road near Maam Cross that quickly leads to wild bogs with abandoned buildings. We experience the deep natural silence there that doesn't lift even with the hardy sheep around. It's a powerful experience!

Day 10- Newgrange, and Knowth, the 5,000-year-old Neolithic Passage Tombs are a wonder. The tours are so interesting. We particularly enjoy our bus driver's story of visiting these sites as a boy. He and his father met the archeologists while picnicking. He feels privileged to work here now. Our GPS is not working; another pilgrimage challenge, or is it an invitation? Fortunately help is again offered, and we return safely to Dublin.

Mamean Pilgrimage Pass

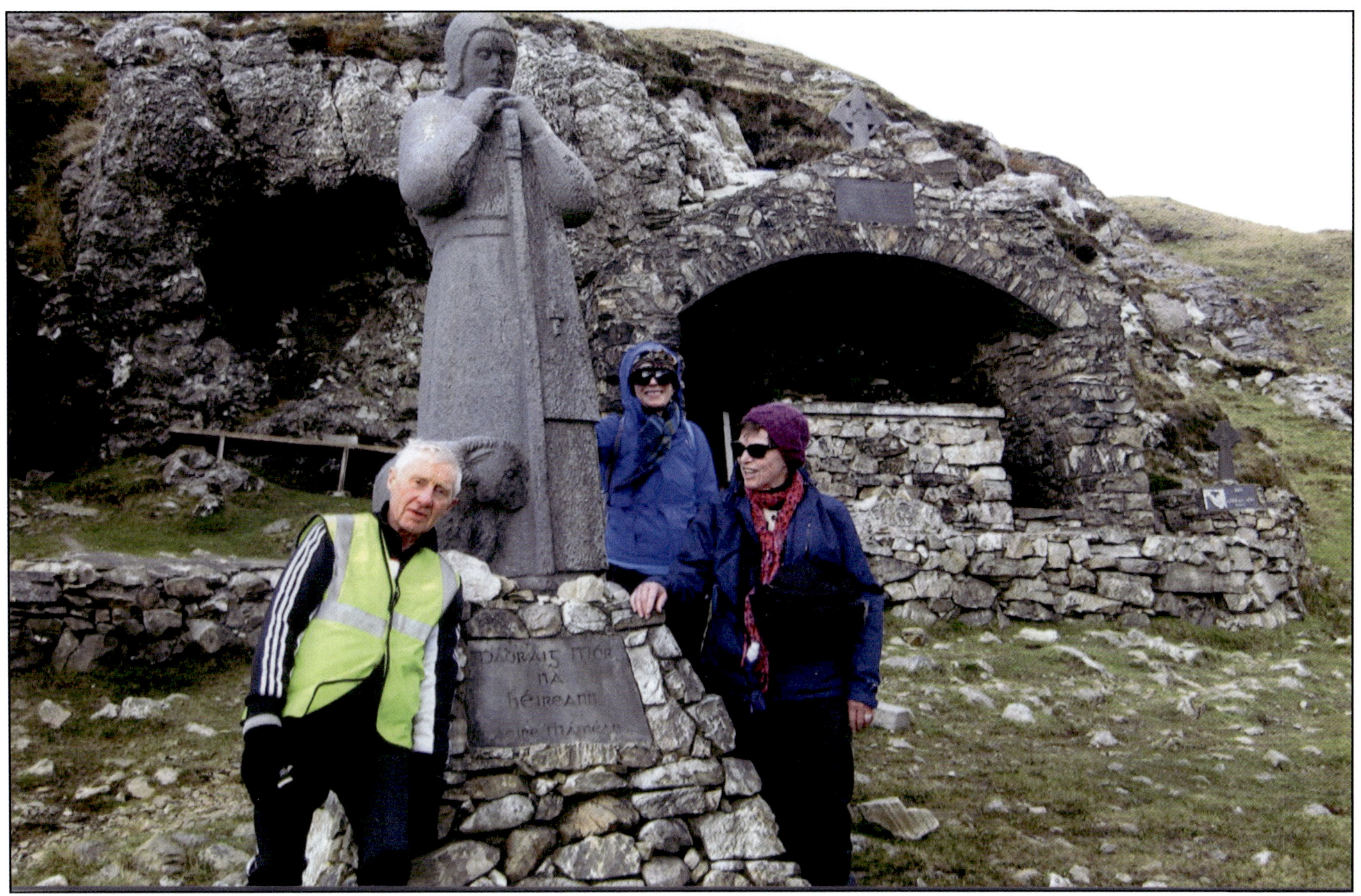

Father Paddy, Patty, and Kathy with St. Patrick.

About the Authors

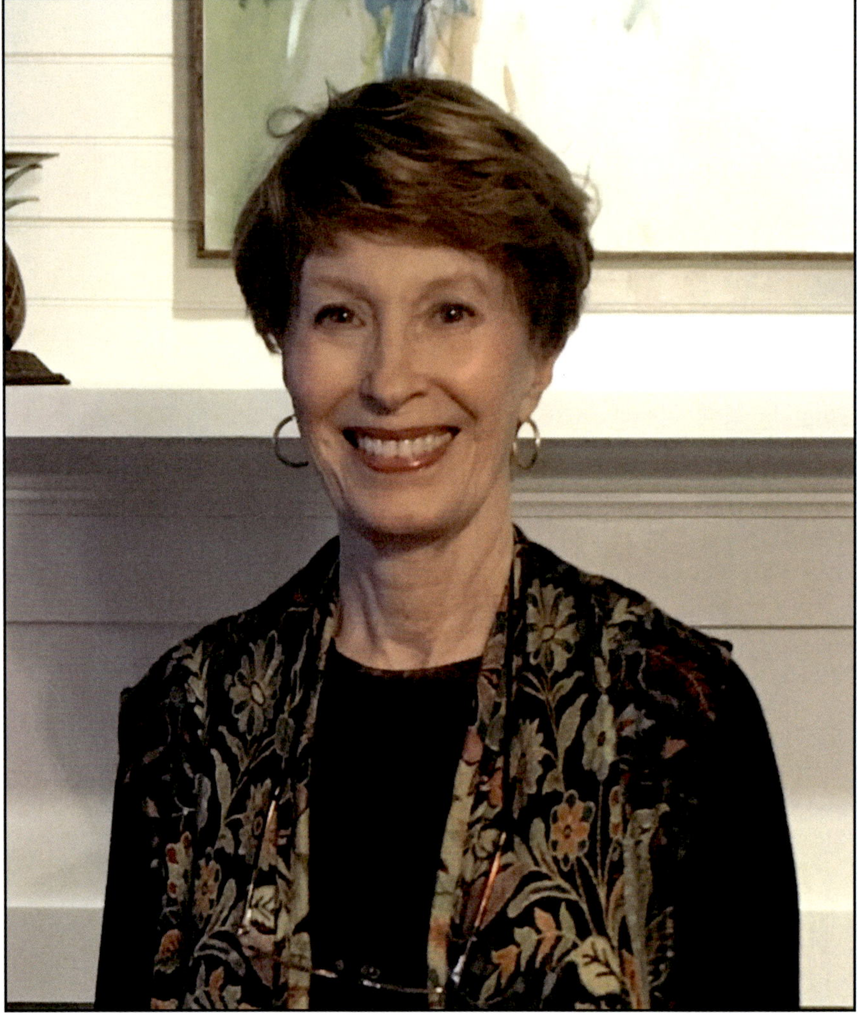

Patty Wheeler Smitherman

Patty is a wife/ mother/ enthusiastic grandmother. She is also a retired Spanish teacher and business owner. Patty has an MA in Spanish Literature and has traveled multiple times to Spanish-speaking countries. She writes, sings, reads, and travels with her husband, Marshall.

Please email her at **pwsmitherman@icloud.com** if you are interested in retreats or workshops.

About the Authors

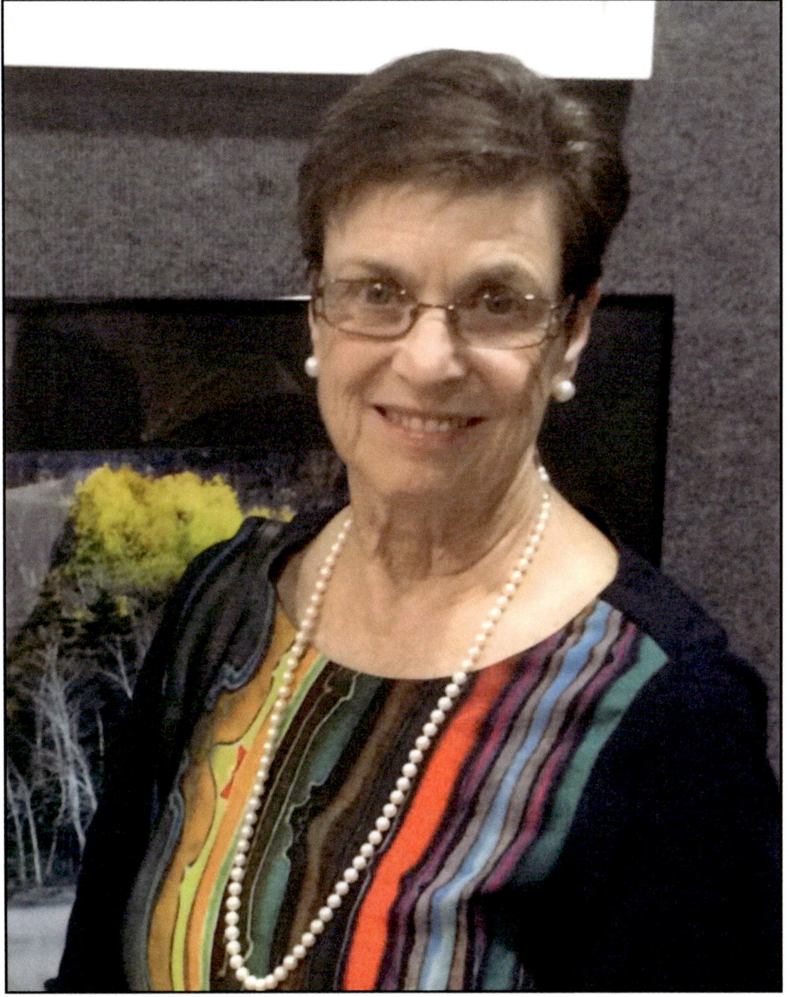

Kathleen Dyer Michaud

Kathy is committed to living life from the inside out. An avid watercolor and mixed media artist, she continues to offer Spiritual Direction at her office. She loves walking and reading especially with her children and grandchildren. Married for 48 years, Kathy and her husband, Fran, enjoy traveling, having friends and family visit, and spending time at the beach.

Please email her at **Michaud.kathy@gmail.com** if you are interested in retreats, workshops or exhibiting these paintings. Follow Kathy on her blog: **kathymichaud.wordpress.com**.

Bibliography

Allen, Pat B. *Art Is a Way of Knowing*. Boston: Shambala, 1995.

Cahill, Thomas. *How the Irish Saved Civilization*. New York: Anchor Books, 1995.

Cousineau, Phil. *The Art of Pilgrimage*. San Francisco: Conari Press, 1998.

Deignan, Kathleen. *Thomas Merton: A Book of Hours*. Notre Dame, Indiana: Sorin Books, 2007.

De Waal, Esther. *The Celtic Way of Prayer: The Recovery of the Religious Imagination*. New York: Doubleday, 1997

_________________ *Every Earthly Blessing, Recovering the Celtic Tradition*. Harrisburg, PA: Morehouse Publishing, 1999.

Earle, Mary C., ed. *Celtic Christian Spirituality: Essential Writings—Annotated & Explained*. Woodstock, Vermont: SkyLight Illuminations, 2011.

Lynch, Tom. *Watercolor Secrets*. Verdi, Nevada: International Artist Publishing Inc., 2000.

Mackey, James P. *An Introduction to Celtic Christianity*. Edinburgh: T&T Clark LTD., 1995.

Newell, John Philip. *The Book of Creation: An Introduction to Celtic Spirituality*. London: Canterbury Press, 1999.

_________________ *Celtic Prayers from Iona*. New York: Paulist Press, 1997.

_________________ *Christ of the Celts: The Healing of Creation*. San Francisco: Josey-Bass. 2008.

_________________ *Listening for the Heartbeat of God*. Society for Promoting Christian Knowledge. London, 1997.

O'Donohue, John. *Beauty*. Great Britain: Bantam Press, 2003.

O'Donohue, John and John Quinn. *Walking on the Pastures of Wonder*. Dublin: Veritas Publications, 2015.

O Duinn, Sean. *Where Three Streams Meet: Celtic Spirituality*. Dublin: The Colomba Press, 2002

Oliver, Mary. *Devotions*. New York: Penguin Random House, 2017.

MacEowen, Frank. *The Mist-Filled Path*. Novarto, CA: New World Library, 2002.

Mollica, Patti. *Color Theory*. Lake Forest, CA: Quatro Publishing Group, 2013.

Somerville, Christopher. "Walk of the Week: Way to Go Mamean Connemara Co Galway." *Irish Independent Newspaper*. Oct. 17, 2009.

Whyte, David. *River Flow*. Langley, WA: Many Rivers Press, 2012.

Woods, Richard, O.P. *Celtic Spirituality*. Bethesda, MA: Now You Know Media, 2011